THE BIRTH OF THE
MONTGOMERY BUS BOYCOTT

Charro Book Co., Inc., Southfield, MI 48034

© 1991 by Charro Book Co., Inc.
ISBN: 0-9629468-0-X

Charro Book Co., Inc.
29777 Telegraph Rd., #2500
Southfield, MI 48034

Published 1991

This publication is available at special discounts for bulk
purchases for sales promotions, premiums, fund-raising, or
educational use. For details, contact the Publisher.

PRINTED IN THE UNITED STATES OF AMERICA

THE BIRTH OF THE MONTGOMERY BUS BOYCOTT

DR. ROBERTA HUGHES WRIGHT

WITH FOREWORD BY

THE HONORABLE

L. DOUGLAS WILDER

GOVERNOR OF THE COMMONWEALTH OF VIRGINIA

CHARRO PRESS, INC.
SOUTHFIELD, MICHIGAN

CONTENTS

FOREWORD

L. Douglas Wilder
Governor of the Commonwealth of Virginia

Nearly two thousand bills have crossed my desk since I was elected Governor of Virginia in 1989. I am directed by our Constitution to review these bills, and am empowered to recommend that they be amended, vetoed, or signed into law. I am not unmindful of the awesome responsibility vested in me by this authority, nor have I lost sight of the historic significance in my performing this function.

Although this nation has come far in recent years in terms of race relations, it is important that we not forget that it was not long ago when African-Americans and other minorities were cast into the long shadows of a discrimination that festered not only within the hearts and souls of many of our brethern, but also within our very own laws.

I have had opportunity to review legislation which affects the civil rights of our citizens in the most fundamental ways. Even as I write, my legislature struggles with the matter of redistricting Virginia's legislative districts in a way that comports with the requirements of the Voting Rights Act. How can one not reflect under these circumstances upon the many men and women who paved the way for the rest of us to be in a position to preside over a process as critical as redistricting. These individuals rose above the fears that would paralyze more tepid souls, and dared to speak for their rights — even if that meant challenging the very fabric of our laws.

Rosa Parks is an individual who, through her indomitable faith in God and her unflagging belief in the dignity of the individual, breathed new life into a people eager to challenge laws which segregated whites and African-Americans who rode on street cars and buses. Dr. Roberta Wright chronicles Ms. Park's historic refusal to sit in the back of a bus in Montgomery, Alabama, in 1955. More importantly, however, Dr. Wright traces the evolution of a people who, as early as 1904, laid the groundwork for organizing successful challenges to segregation in public transportation.

I cannot stress enough the importance of learning from history, and this history in particular, that there is no one person who alone can claim the mantle of having advanced the plight of the outcast and downtrodden. That mantle has been borne collectively by the thousands of souls who had infinite faith in the possibilities of individuals, and in particular, African-Americans, to overcome what appeared to be insurmountable obstacles. *The Birth of the Montgomery Bus Boycott* is a living tribute to all those who carried the mantle.

L. Douglas Wilder
Governor of the Commonwealth of Virginia
Office of the Governor
Richmond, Virginia

ACKNOWLEDGEMENTS

This book was a labour of love; for I became enamored, so to speak, with the players whose real life activism was a pleasure to set forth and to witness, albeit second-hand. The generous assistance of so many people made all of this possible, and a joy of accomplishment. Initial thanks go to my family, all of whom were helpful and supportive in recording the events of *The Birth of the Montgomery Bus Boycott.*

Special thanks to my husband, Charles H. Wright, M.D., who provided his twenty-year old taped interviews with Rosa; her husband, Raymond; her mother, Mrs. Leona McCauley and Ed Nixon, the Montgomery leader who signed for Rosa's release from prison on December 1, 1955. Charles also made it possible for us to spend considerable time in San Juan, Puerto Rico's beautiful Isla Verde. Composition seems easier when one can occasionally look up and see the spectacular condominiums lining the sandy beaches of the beautiful Atlantic Ocean and the blue, blue sky filled with birds competing for airspace with the steady flow of jet planes to and from the nearby airport.

OUR CHILDREN AND GRANDCHILDREN deserve special acknowledgement. We transformed daughter Barbara

Allen Finch's Christmas Eve family dinner into a critique session of the book as I outlined parts of the then incomplete manuscript. Helpful comments were received from Dolores and Dave Harold; Susan and Julius Watson and son, Alan; Judy Griffin; Blythe Allen (Spelman College) and Brett Allen (Howard University); James McGowan; Walter Williams; and my son, Wilbur Hughes III, who was often pressed into service. Also helpful were family members Stephanie and William Griggs, and Louisa and Carla Wright, M.D. of Milwaukee. The experience gained by William in publishing his recent book, *The Megalight Connection,* was passed along, freely, and was of inestimable value.

IN JANUARY 1991, a family reunion in Cleveland, Ohio, provided an opportunity for more critical appraisal, especially that of cousin, Lewis Wright, whose suggestions for the opening were timely and imaginative.

I am deeply indebted to Detroit artist, Leroy Foster, for permission to use his portrait of Rosa, her husband and her mother. Thanks are extended to Dr. Marion Moore, executive director of the Museum of African American History and her staff for providing the color print included in the book.

SPECIAL TRIBUTE goes to others who gave invaluable assistance: Mrs. Thelma Glass, Mrs. Johnnie Carr, and Cecil St. Clair of Montgomery, Alabama; Mrs. Marymal Dryden of Atlanta, Georgia, who was always ready to answer my many questions; Attorney James Bearden of Washington, D.C.; Eloise and Robert Shannon of Detroit, and Dr. Iwok Essein and his wife, Dr. Joyce Essein of Atlanta. The Essein's spacious and beautiful Niskey Lake Trail home was generously offered and graciously received as our headquarters on three trips to Atlanta while I absorbed some of Atlanta's resources of knowledge, especially at the Martin Luther King, Jr., Center for Nonviolent Change.

SIMILARLY, I want to pay special tribute to Dr. and Mrs. Isaac Graves of Detroit. Olga Graves, a Richmond, Virginia native, was very helpful with the Virginia portion of the manuscript. Also helpful were Samuel Madden, William Mitchell, and Oliver W. Hill of Richmond. A bouquet of orchids goes to Christina Barbara Hughes' maternal grandparents, Evelyn and Ben Hawkins, for searching Virginia's archives and sending that important 1904 story of Richmond. The Richmond Public Library and Sarah J. Huggins of the Virginia State Library and Archives contributed by sending material. Also, thanks to Troy and Howard Moss, relatives of Richmond's Mitchell family.

SPECIAL THANKS to Professor Roger A. Fischer of the University of Minnesota, for allowing me to use his fascinating article on the New Orleans boycott; to the University of Tennessee for permission to use quotes from Jo Ann Robinson's book; and to the other authors who are listed in the endnotes and the bibliography; to Dr. Norman McRae, historian, who sent material written by Vernon Jarrett, Chicago columnist; to Dr. William Anderson, civil rights activist who provided helpful suggestions; to Aretha and Joseph Marshall for their assistance; to the Detroit Sophisticates for their comments on the proposed book cover; and to Charles Alexander for his assistance.

THE BIRTH OF THE MONTGOMERY BUS BOYCOTT inaugurates the CHARRO BOOK COMPANY. This is the first in a series of publications designed to fill in some of the omissions and correct published distortions, inadvertent and otherwise, of the black experience.

Rosa & Raymond Parks and Rosa's mother, Mrs. Leona McCauley

artist, Leroy Foster

INTRODUCTION

December 1, 1955, was a cloudy, rather dull day; the temperature was above freezing. The cool, damp weather with a threat of rain, was a proper setting for the human drama that was about to unfold in downtown Montgomery, Alabama.

Mrs. Rosa Parks, a seamstress at the Montgomery Fair department store, put aside her sewing paraphernalia and, as usual, left the store. A bit tired, she was anxious to get home. At that moment, she had no thought that before reaching home she would trigger a series of events that would not only change her life, but the course of the nation's history, as well.

As the Cleveland Avenue bus approached, the one Mrs. Parks normally took to get to her home at 634 Cleveland Court on the west side of town, she could see that it was already crowded and decided to wait for the next one. She crossed the street and, as was her custom, went into Lee's Cut Rate drug store to shop. She purchased a few items and considered buying an electric heating pad to put on her neck and shoulders but changed her mind and left the store.

As she returned to the Court Square stop, another bus came along. It was not full, and she thought that if she caught this one she might be able to sit down. As the patrons rushed to get on the bus, Mrs. Parks recognized the driver as one who, several years before, had evicted her because she had refused to put her fare in the front fare box and go around to the back door to reenter the bus.

She took the only remaining vacant seat next to the aisle,

immediately behind the "lily-white" section. Mrs. Parks clearly recalls that, "The seat I took was in the colored section." She sat down beside a black man, holding her bag in her lap. Directly across the aisle from her sat two black women.

At the third stop, several white passengers boarded the bus, filling their section. One white man was left standing. The driver looked around and, speaking to the first row of black passengers, demanded, "You let him have those front seats!" The four black passengers knew exactly what the driver meant. This scenario had been played out hundreds of times before, but in different circumstances and with different characters.

The driver was asking all four blacks to stand up to accommodate this one white man, to enforce the requirements of the Alabama state law. None of the blacks said anything, nor did they move. Referring to the four seats where Mrs. Parks and the others were sitting, the bus driver again demanded the seats saying, "You all better make it light on yourselves and let me have those seats."

Responding to this threatening command, three of the four black passengers got up; but Mrs. Parks only moved her legs so that the man in her window seat could pass. He moved into the aisle and stood with the two black women.

The bus driver, J.S. Blake, left his seat, hovered over Mrs. Parks, still seated, and asked if she was going to get up. Mrs. Parks answered, "No." She had no intention of moving. Increasingly insistent before the full audience of the crowded bus, he thundered, "If you don't get up, I'm gonna call the police." That threat usually got prompt obedience. Not this time. Quietly, Mrs. Parks advised him to go ahead and make his call.[1]

Thus began what became one of the longest and most successful civil rights protests, in the history of the Movement. My focus is primarily on the first four days — December 1 through December 5, 1955 — one hundred momentous hours.

This document is certainly not the first word on this historic event and will not be the last. Due to the passage of time, paucity of authentic documentation and failing, selective memories of the survivors, a statement that represents a general consensus of what happened, is not possible. After reading most, if not all of the available accounts, reviewing taped interviews, some of which are more than twenty years old, and talking with many of the survivors, the following account is as accurate a report of the Birth of a Boycott as was possible.

Suffice it to say that each participant, when called upon, stepped forth with alacrity and discharged his or her responsibility with selfless courage, producing a symphony of community cooperation that changed this nation's history.

It is my goal to collect the data and retell the story of the beginning of this remarkable saga in such a sequence that the courage, confidence and heroism of the participants can be clearly seen and adequately appreciated. As is true in all such struggles, three factors are of paramount importance in determining who wins or loses:

The Arena

The Armaments

The Adversaries

The Adversary who can choose all three is sure to emerge the winner. If two are chosen, success is still possible. When the enemy chooses two or more of these options, the chances for success are minimal to non-existent.

In this case, Montgomery, Alabama, revered by some as "The Cradle of the Confederacy", was the arena. For those of us for whom the Confederacy is not a celebratory event, Montgomery is better remembered as the incubator of the Civil Rights Movement. It was there that the idea of a Montgomery Bus Boycott was conceived, born, bred and grew to become the launching pad for a ten-year movement that changed the course of this nation's history, for the better. It became the model for other freedom movements around the world.

As luck would have it, for all practical purposes the Civil Rights Movement began in Montgomery with the 1955 Bus Boycott, and ended ten years later in Montgomery, at the end of the Selma to Montgomery march, in March of 1965. Thus, Montgomery was the arena for much of the action during this Decade of Destiny.

More than a century earlier, in 1846, Montgomery had become important enough to wrest the state capital away from the city of Tuscaloosa. And in 1851, the capitol building located at the head of Dexter Avenue, was partially constructed. Each of the city's ninety, well-to-do, planter families as early as 1830, owned at least $5,000 in property. The per capita wealth of all free persons was more than $700.00, a figure never attained by the United States as a whole, during the entire ante-bellum period.

Montgomery never had the raucous shoot-em-up stage that some cities experienced. With a frontier facade, it was a decorous city where gaming devices were forbidden, slaves carefully controlled, and a nine o'clock curfew faithfully observed. While keeping tight rein over lawless elements, its leaders preferred to humiliate offenders by tarring and feathering them or dunking them in the river, rather than using more extreme measures. No one was executed during Montgomery's first decade; only four murders were recorded between 1830 and 1840.

But as its population grew, Montgomery, too, partook of Alabama's addiction to violence. Although the state law forbade the carrying of concealed weapons, Alabama ranked fifth among the thirty-one states in 1850, in the number of accidental deaths from gunshot. This casual use of firearms and bowie knives was attributed to the marked tendency on the part of Montgomerians, Alabamians and southerners generally, to settle disputes quickly, individually and outside the law. An unwritten code sanctioned the white man's right to defend himself from insult or assault, without fear of punishment.

Violence also stemmed from the subjugation of a black majority by a white minority, increasingly fearful of general slave uprisings or individual acts of vengeance. The slave population exceeded that of whites in Montgomery county as early as 1830; by 1860, blacks outnumbered whites two to one.

Sons of Montgomery's pioneer planters adopted the profession of law so enthusiastically that Montgomery, like other black-belt counties, swarmed with attorneys. The ranks of physicians were almost as crowded. Such men were not only heirs to the plantation system, but to the conviction that political control was their natural right. Although they might criticize their own institutions, they brooked no censure from outsiders, believing that only they understood the problems of their society. Proud, successful and accustomed to leadership, this compact group, closely interwoven by marriage and kinship, marshalled its talents to secure its position.[2]

Although this coterie united against outsiders, it divided internally for three decades. Politics, a subject of interest in Montgomery second only to cotton prices, ran the gamut from Jacksonian Democracy to Union Whiggery, from broad construction to nullification. But the rising challenge of abolitionism forced Montgomerians to choose between Henry H. Hilliard, who pleaded for harmony within the Union and William Lowndes Yancey, who electrified listeners with his cry, "Patriotism begins at home!"

By 1860, the firebrand secessionist, Yancey, had prevailed. Montgomery County, like every other county in the Black Belt and all but one in central and southern Alabama, voted to secede from the Union by such thumping majorities that reluctant elements in the hill country and Wiregrass counties, were overwhelmed. Convinced that the status quo could be maintained by abandoning the Union, ninety-four percent of Montgomery's voters cast ballots for secession, the first state to do so, making sure that their city should become "the Cradle of the Confederacy."[3]

On February 4, 1861, forty-two delegates from South Carolina, Georgia, Mississippi, Louisiana, Florida and Alabama, met in Montgomery and elected the Mississippian, Jefferson Davis, to the presidency of the Confederate States of America. In his Inaugural address, Davis endorsed slavery "as necessary to self-preservation."

Thus the social climate and political control of Alabama were set to last through the Civil War, the Reconstruction period and the end of the 19th century. When these disciples of white supremacy left the scene, they passed their mantles of authority on to succeeding generations. One such successor was the Montgomery bus driver, who on December 1, 1955, ordered three black women and one black man, all paying passengers, to stand in the aisle so that one white could sit.

Earlier, in 1900, when segregation was first imposed on Montgomery's streetcars, blacks mounted a summer boycott forcing a modification of the segregation law to specify that no person had to give up one's seat unless another seat was available. In 1906, a more stringent Montgomery city ordinance went beyond the state's jim crow law and mandated separate buses for blacks and whites.[4]

The Armaments were the indomitable will of an oppressed people to be free, on the one hand, and the enormously oppressive resources of the racist antagonists, on the other.

One of the Adversaries was a rag-tag, unorganized but courageous band of black citizens who threw their usual caution to the wind and challenged the well-armed, confident, and condescending guardians of status quo. The white adversaries had every reason to believe that this confrontation would be brief and the walls of bigotry would remain intact as usual.

Certainly history was on their side. The altar to white

supremacy was firmly established on these shores with the arrival of the first European, Christopher Columbus, 500 years ago. Since that time, sacrificial lambs to that idol have been demanded from all non-Europeans, in foreign as well as domestic transactions.

So when James F. Blake, the Montgomery city bus driver, demanded that four blacks, three women and one man, stand so that one white man could sit, he was following a script that was older than the nation. Three of the supplicants bowed to that goddess and stood up. The fourth, Mrs. Rosa Parks, did what few others before her dared do; she defied the conventional assumption that her blackness was a badge of inferiority. She decided, then and there, that her days of penance for her color were over, no matter what it would cost. She just sat there.

The keeper of the flame, the bus driver, did what he was trained to do — park his bus and seek reinforcements to deal with this threat to the status quo. Although every passenger on that full bus had his or her agenda that evening, all became subordinated to the urgent need to protect the citadel of bigotry, racial segregation.

The bus driver's departure for help began an incredible journey where you, the reader, will meet some remarkable people, all of whom played crucial roles in the unfolding drama. Come along with me for a formal introduction to some of them.

Rosa McCauley Parks — Rosa was born on February 4, 1913, in Tuskegee, Alabama. At an early age, she, her brother, Sylvester and her mother moved to Pine Level, Alabama, a rural community twenty miles from Montgomery. Rosa later moved to Montgomery, where she lived until 1957, when she moved to Detroit, Michigan.

Soft spoken and gentle, Rosa was and is a quiet person of great dignity whose reserve belies a steel-like determination. Although she had no children of her own, all through the years she worked diligently with young people, assisting them over difficult hurdles encountered in their lives. For twelve years as secretary of the Montgomery branch of the NAACP, she spent considerably more than job time encouraging and assisting disfranchised blacks. Her role in the Montgomery Bus Boycott was crucial to its birth and remains a high point in the Civil Rights Movement, generally.

James F. Blake — Blake, the bus driver, was an employee of the Montgomery City Lines. He did what he had to do when his white authority was challenged by a black passenger. This was not Mrs. Parks' first abrasive encounter with this driver. In that earlier confrontation, Blake allowed her to enter the bus only to pay her fare. Due to the crowding in the front, he ordered her to exit and reenter the bus by the back door. Before she could reenter, Blake drove away, a common misfortune for many black passengers.

Little is known or was written about Blake. The December 2, 1955, *Montgomery Advertiser* reported: J.F. Blake, 27 N. Lewis Street, in notifying police, said, "a Negro woman, sitting in the section reserved for Whites, refused to move to the Negro section."

Leona and James McCauley — Rosa's mother, Leona, had been a teacher and her father, James, a carpenter. They separated when Rosa was quite young and she lived with her mother, thereafter. Mrs. McCauley had a strong influence on Rosa, teaching her the sense of self-respect and self-pride. She took part in the decision that Rosa would take her case to court.

During the boycott, Mrs. McCauley protected her daughter as best she could, intercepting hate calls and poison pen letters and "keeping her food warm until she could get home," remembered Mrs. McCauley during a 1970 interview.

Raymond Parks — Raymond Parks met Rosa in 1931, and they married that following year. A barber, he was also active with the NAACP and other community organizations. During the 1930s, he helped to raise funds for the defendants in the Scottsboro Boys case in which nine blacks were convicted on the basis of skimpy evidence and perjured testimony, of raping two white women in northern Alabama.

After the boycott started, Mr. Parks tried to work at Maxwell Field, a military air base; but the concessionaire and others, continually harassed him. He returned to the city in search of a job, but his former barber shop had closed. The cost of renting a chair at a new shop was $12.00 per week. Since haircuts were sixty-five cents each, it was difficult to make a living. This community backlash was a significant factor in causing Raymond and Rosa to move to Detroit, in 1957.

Edgar Daniel Nixon — E.D. Nixon was born in 1895, in Montgomery, Alabama. His father was a baptist minister and his mother a maid. On his own by the age of fourteen, he started working at menial jobs such as baggage room porter at the Union Station. His industry led to his being hired as a sleeping car porter.

Nixon became seriously involved in community action work in the late 1920s, after two children drowned while swimming in a Montgomery drainage ditch. He organized an unsuccessful drive to build a swimming pool for blacks.

Nixon took the lead in many civil rights causes and was active with numerous organizations. The Montgomery Welfare League and the Montgomery Voters League were among the many groups that profited from his support. He was a former head of the local NAACP as well as the state chapter of the NAACP.

Several times previously, Nixon had been called to help organize a boycott of the bus system. Each time, he studied the incident and the circumstances surrounding it and decided against any action. With Rosa Parks he was ready to move. His role, as we shall see, was crucial.

Nixon continued in the struggle for freedom until his death at the age of eighty-seven. So that coming generations will never forget Mr. Nixon's many contributions to the fight for Freedom and Justice, especially during the Montgomery Bus Boycott, a historic marker has been placed on his house in Montgomery.

Fred D. Gray — Attorney Fred Gray, a native son of Montgomery's black community, graduated from Alabama State College in Montgomery, and from the school of law at Cleveland's Case Western Reserve University. He opened his law office in Montgomery in 1954, the year before the Bus Boycott.

Along with his partner, Attorney Charles D. Langford, he had already represented the NAACP in several civil rights cases. He became involved in the Montgomery Bus Boycott from its earliest beginnings and stayed with it until the end, as legal advisor to the Montgomery Improvement Association. Presently, he is a senior member of the Gray, Langford, Sapp and McGowan law firm, with offices in Montgomery and Tuskegee.

Virginia & Clifford Durr — Clifford Durr was a liberal white attorney who had returned to Montgomery from Washington, D.C., in 1951, where he had served as a member of the Federal Communications Commission. He and his wife, Virginia, were sympathetic to the causes of blacks, in general, and to the bus litigation, in particular. Such loyalties did not endear them to the white community and Durr's legal practice suffered significantly.

It was Attorney Durr who suggested, in February 1956, that a new case should be filed in federal court, challenging Alabama's segregation law.

Virginia Durr, the daughter of a Birmingham minister, knew Rosa well and followed her activities with the NAACP. Reportedly, she encouraged Mrs. Parks to attend the Highlander Folk School to study techniques of civil rights protests.

Ralph David Abernathy — Reverend Abernathy, pastor of Montgomery's First Baptist Church (colored), was well known and highly respected by the other Baptist ministers, as secretary of the Baptist Ministerial Alliance. Only 29 years of age at that time, he had already built a reputation as a hard worker and a good preacher. Later, his popularity and hard work propelled him into the office of the director of programs of the Montgomery Improvement Association. He was well chosen by E.D. Nixon to recruit other ministers to attend a meeting to discuss the Bus Boycott.

Martin Luther King, Jr. — Rev. King was born in Atlanta, Georgia, on January 15, 1929. After graduating from Atlanta's Morehouse college, with honors, he attended the Crozer Theological Seminary in Pennsylvania. It was there that he heard Rev. Mordicai Johnson, president of Howard University, speak of Mahatma Gandhi and nonviolence. He went on to Boston University to earn his Ph.D. degree, in Philosophy, and was influenced by that great theologian and mystic, Howard Thurman.

The membership of the Dexter Avenue Baptist Church called Rev. King to the pastorate in 1954. Like many others who seem to have been placed in Montgomery by destiny, King's prior preparation served him well for his calling to lead the Montgomery Bus Boycott. At Morehouse, Crozer Seminary and Boston University, as will be explained later, he was exposed to influences that shaped his life and prepared him for world leadership.

King's leadership in the Civil Rights Movement began when he was 26 years of age and continued without pause until his assassination in 1968. His speech, on the evening of December 5, 1955, accepting leadership of the Bus Boycott, propelled the campaign into its successful 381-day orbit.

H.H. Hubbard — Reverend Hubbard, pastor of the Bethel Baptist Church, was well known for the aid he gave to Montgomery's victimized and needy black citizens. Since he was Mr. Nixon's pastor, it was natural for Nixon to turn to him for assistance in mobilizing the ministers. Hubbard's resources were enhanced through his office as president of the Baptist Ministerial Alliance, the union of all black Baptist ministers.

Edgar French — Reverend French, pastor of the Hilliard Chapel, AME Zion Church, served as corresponding secretary of the Montgomery Improvement Association. Active from the beginning of the campaign, he was instrumental in drawing up the Resolutions of Demands that were later presented to the people for approval.

A.W. Wilson — Reverend Wilson, pastor of Holt Street Baptist Church, was described as a successful, middle-aged minister with a "tough constitution." He demanded true loyalty from his congregation. His west-side church and congregation were among the largest and most modern in the city. He readily agreed to host the crucial, do-or-die, mass meeting on December 5th, after the successful first-day of the Bus Boycott.

William J. Powell — Reverend Powell, the well-known pastor of Old Ship A.M.E. Zion Church, was born in the small town of Crenshaw, Alabama, about 25 miles from Montgomery. His family moved to Birmingham when he was 7 years old. There he received his primary and secondary education. He continued his theological education at Livingstone College's Hood Seminary, in Salisbury, North Carolina. He began preaching in Birmingham; but like Attorney Gray and Rev. King, he came to Montgomery in 1954. Old Ship Church is the oldest and most revered church in Montgomery's black community.

Rev. Powell's well-known organizing skills were put to great use as head of the MIA's Transportation committee. It was under his guidance that the taxi cab companies and various other forms of transport were coordinated to provide maximum service despite the hostility and sabotage efforts of the establishment. By and large, his organization was able to provide a remarkable service to the besieged community for the same ten cents that the buses charged.

L. Roy Bennett — Reverend Bennett, pastor of Mount Zion A.M.E. Zion Church, was president of the Interdenominational

Ministerial Alliance, whose membership included almost all of the black ministers in Montgomery, regardless of their denomination. He was the natural selection of presiding officer at the first meeting of ministers at the Dexter Avenue Baptist Church, on December 2, 1955.

Bennett's high-handed, autocratic method of conducting the meeting, however, caused some of the ministers to leave the church. Fortunately, Rev. Abernathy took charge and allowed the other ministers to share in the policy-making that ensued. A disruption that early in the planning would have been catastrophic.

Jo Ann Gibson Robinson — Jo Ann Robinson moved to Montgomery, late in the summer of 1949, at the age of 33, to join the English Department of the all-black Alabama State Teachers College. She was born in Culloden, Georgia, twenty-five miles from Macon. The 12th child of Owen and Dollie Gibson, she graduated as valedictorian, from high school in Macon. She earned her bachelor's degree at Fort Valley State College and her masters in English at Atlanta University, both in Georgia. Her marriage to Wilbur Robinson ended after the death in infancy of their first and only child.

Robinson taught in Texas, before coming to Alabama. Through her connections at Alabama State College and her affiliation with the Women's Political Council, Mrs. Robinson played a crucial role in the launching and perpetuation of the Montgomery Bus Boycott.

Lawrence D. Reddick — L.D. Reddick, chairman of the History Department at Alabama State, had a scholarly interest in preserving historical documents for future generations. Reddick worked diligently during the boycott, attending the Monday night meetings and assisting whenever and however he could. He helped to chronicle the events of the campaign through "The Bus Boycott," in Montgomery, printed in *Dissent,* spring, 1956, and *Crusader Without Violence,* a biography of Dr. King, published in 1959.

He was the first professor affected when in 1959-1960, a special State Committee was sent to investigate the role of the college's professors in the Bus Boycott. Reddick was tried in absentia, without a hearing or the opportunity to defend himself. He was found guilty and ordered to leave the Alabama College campus and the city of Montgomery. Guilt feelings still linger about the way he was mishandled.

Rufus Lewis — Rufus "Coach" Lewis was at first, a professor at Alabama State College. Later, he resigned to become a full-time businessman. He and his family are well respected in the community and were often approached for advice in operating businesses. Lewis was president of the Citizens Steering Committee, a voter registration organization.

Lewis owned a private nightclub for blacks and had a rule that only registered voters could become members. His philosophy was often expressed as "a voteless people is a hopeless people." Lewis, along with Alphonso Campbell, was a member of the MIA's Transportation Committee and did a superb job in mapping out routes for drivers to pick up and discharge boycotters.

James E. Pierce — James Pierce, professor of science at Alabama State, was a key, black, Montgomery activist. He was secretary of the Montgomery Improvement League, one of the many civic groups existing in the city at that time. Pierce worked closely with Rufus Lewis, tackling the problem of securing franchise permits from the city commissioners to operate jitneys for black riders.

Other ministers who played important roles in the boycott were: The Rev. W.F. Alford, pastor of Beulah Baptist Church; Rev. Uriah J. Fields, pastor of the Bell Street Baptist Church, and the first recording secretary of the MIA; Rev. Vernon Johns, former pastor of the Dexter Avenue Baptist Church before King's arrival; Rev. Robert S. Graetz, a young white minister at the black Lutheran Church. He actively supported the boycott and suffered constant harassment from the white community, as a result; Rev. S.D. Seay, who had years of experience acquired by fighting for the rights of blacks; Rev. B.J. Simms, who was a college professor as well as pastor of a Baptist church in Tuskegee; Rev. Joshua Hayes, who assisted Rev. Powell with the negotiations for the taxi franchises; the Rev. Dr. M.C. Cleveland, pastor of Day Street Baptist Church; Rev. I.H. Cherry, who served as chief dispatcher at a downtown parking lot, during the boycott; and Rev. Theodore Jemison, who led the bus boycott in Baton Rouge, Louisiana, and gave invaluable assistance to the MIA.

There were other major participants, but it is impossible to name all of them. Together, they represented a significant number from all segments of the black citizenry. Among these were Mrs. Portia Trenholm, wife of Dr. H. Councill Trenholm, the president of Alabama State College. A member of the music faculty, she was helpful to the WPC, particularly as a liaison between the organization and the college administration.

Mrs. Irene West, widow of a prominent dentist, Dr. A.W. West, Sr., recruited heads of the Women's Federated Clubs and other civic leaders. She spent a good portion of her life fighting for first class citizenship for blacks. She was active in clubs and social organizations that promoted the cause of education throughout the years. Although in her seventies at the time of the boycott, she chauffeured persons trying to reach employment and gave other services to the cause.

Frank Massey, talented and able youth leader, organized brigades, helped to distribute literature and contributed, greatly; Jeremiah Howard, proprietor of the Howard and Howard Funeral Home and owner of Good Service Taxi Company, one of the larger cab fleets in the city; Erna Dungee, able worker who served as financial secretary of the MIA; Thelma Glass, an ardent worker and active member of the WPC; Mrs. Georgia Gilmore, solid, energetic boycott participant and supporter; Mr. Aubrey

Williams, one of the few white liberals involved in the day-to-day operation. He was publisher of the *Southern Farmer* but lost all of his advertising when he became a supporter of the MIA; Mrs. Johnnie Carr, active supporter who later became president of the MIA. She was a long-time friend and classmate of Rosa Parks at Mrs. White's school; Richard Harris, a black pharmacist, who helped Rev. Cherry as dispatcher and was a great asset with the transportation during the boycott; Dr. Moses A. Jones, boycott activist and later, second vice president of MIA; and Coretta Scott King, who assisted in the fund-raising for MIA.

These were not the first persons to challenge the system of racial segregation in public transportation. The most celebrated challenger to segregation in public transportation, of all times, was Homer A. Plessy.

ONE

The Setting

Rosa Parks, in 1955, was traveling on the Cleveland Avenue bus in Montgomery, Alabama. Sixty years previously, Homer A. Plessy was aboard a train traveling from New Orleans to Covington, Louisiana. A kinship of spirit, a kinship of determination brought them together in an unexpected manner.

In reality, of course, those two never met. Homer Plessy, in 1892, held a first class train ticket but was ordered to ride in the "colored" coach. Mr. Plessy, like Rosa, refused to leave his seat. The conductor summoned police power as Blake did many years later, to help manage Mrs. Parks. Mr. Plessy was removed, arrested and in 1896, brought before the court in the celebrated case, Plessy v. Ferguson.[1]

Mr. Plessy asked the Louisiana high court to prohibit Judge Ferguson from hearing the case. He alleged that Louisiana's segregation law was unconstitutional because it violated the Thirteenth Amendment,[2] and in particular, because it denied him equal protection of the laws, guaranteed by the Fourteenth Amendment.[3]

The Louisiana Supreme Court held that a state law ordering racial separation of passengers, on a railroad train, did not offend the equal protection clause of the Fourteenth Amendment as long as equal facilities were provided for both whites and Negroes. Mr. Plessy then asked the United States Supreme Court to intervene.

Justice Henry Billings Brown, the first of Michigan's two Supreme Court Justices, wrote the Court's seven-to-one majority

17

opinion which agreed that the Fourteenth Amendment was "undoubtedly to enforce the absolute equality of the two races before the law. But," he added, "in the nature of things, it could not have been intended to abolish distinction based on color, or to enforce social equality."

After much discourse, Justice Brown expounded on what he said was the fallacy in Mr. Plessy's complaint, "We consider the underlying weakness of the plaintiff's argument was the assumption that the enforced separation of the two races stamps the Colored race with a badge of inferiority. If this be so," he said, "it is not by reason of anything found in the Act, but solely because the Colored race chooses to put that assumption upon it."

Justice John M. Harlan, a southerner from Kentucky, was alone in his dissent. He scorned the rationalization that the equal-and- separate law was passed with any concern for the rights of Negroes. He wrote that he could see clearly that in "the view of the Constitution, in the eyes of the law, there is in this country no superior, dominant ruling class of citizens. The law," he said, "regards man as man, and takes no account of his color when his civil rights, as guaranteed by the supreme law of the land, are involved."

Justice Harlan accurately foresaw that the separate-but-equal doctrine would not be confined to railroads, but he could not forecast the lengths to which it would be carried. Even Justice Harlan could not predict that the time would come when "streetcar" segregation would be the universal rule in the entire South, to be abandoned only after the sensational Negro boycott in Montgomery, Alabama almost 65 years later.

Justice Harlan had a final word for those who insisted that segregation statutes would assure racial harmony. "The Negro," he said, "objects, and ought never to cease objecting to the proposition that citizens of white and black races can be adjudged criminals because they sit or claim the right to sit, in the same public coach on a public highway."

Although the immediate and intended effect of the Plessy decision was that it sanctioned jim crow laws,[4] the wound was far deeper than that. It grafted a color-caste system onto the amended Constitution, a result achieved by vesting the states and, presumably, the national government, with the power to classify their citizens and residents on the basis of race.

With his color as a badge of inferiority, among white supremacists, the Negro faced all manners of difficulties. Assaulted and beaten by a Ku Klux Klan[5] mob intent on keeping him in his place, he might seek redress through laws passed by Congress to put down Klan violence. If so, he would be told, ultimately, by the Supreme Court that the laws on which he depended were void.

He was told that the right he claimed was not an attribute of his natural citizenship, but of his state citizenship. He would also be told that the Fourteenth Amendment did not empower Congress to protect rights flowing from state citizenship and that he must turn to his state for protection. In practice, the hostile state would not protect him.

Prior to the end of the Civil War, the legitimacy of white supremacy was certified by the Dred Scott decision, Dred Scott v. Sandford,[6] written by Chief Justice Roger B. Taney, in 1857. The court declared that the descendants of Africans who were imported into this country and sold as slaves were not included nor intended to be included under the word "citizens" in the Constitution and could not claim any of the rights and privileges which the Constitution instrument provided for and secured to citizens of the United States.

After the war and with passage of the Thirteenth Amendment obliterating slavery, and the Fourteenth Amendment offering the constitutional rights of citizenship to Negroes, the supremacists demanded new assurance that their supremacy status was unchanged. As states rightists, they began to mobilize before the war was over, and were able to defeat Reconstruction and hold democracy hostage. The Plessy v. Ferguson decision was just the federal government's capitulation to the South's merciless onslaught.

Before a decade had passed, in 1905, the case Berea College v. Kentucky[7] brought to light a new and more restrictive interpretation of the Constitution. Berea College was established in Kentucky in 1854 and incorporated under Kentucky law in 1859. After the Civil War, students were admitted without reference to race or color. By 1904, it had 753 white and 174 Negro students. It was a Christian school and the students and faculty practiced Christianity as they understood the religion. However the Kentucky legislature enacted a statute, effective July 15, 1904, forbidding the maintenance of any "school, college or institution where persons of the white and Negro race are both received as pupils of instruction."

Kentucky's statute, forbidding the teaching of white and Negro students, at the same school at the same time was a broad one and applied to "any person, corporation, or association of persons maintaining or operating any school, college or institution." In the Supreme Court in 1908, Justice David J. Brewer sidestepped the real question. He did not deal with the great constitutional issue before the Court, that of whether or not a state could classify its citizens on the basis of race and forbid their voluntary association for innocent purposes on the basis of that classification.

Justice Harlan dissented to the majority opinion as he had done in previous, similar cases. He argued that the Supreme Court should directly meet and decide the broad question presented and should adjudge whether the statute is or is not unconstitutional.

Justice Harlan warned that Kentucky would regard the

decision as a blanket endorsement of the principle that "the teaching of white and black pupils at the same time, even in a private institution, is a crime against that Commonwealth no matter whether the school was conducted by a corporation or by a private person or an association of persons." The warning became a reality. Soon interracial teaching ceased in all Kentucky schools.

The disappointed Berea College faculty and students did the best they could. In the fall of 1905, they bore transportation expenses of more than one hundred of the 174 Negro students forced to transfer to Negro schools. The white students expressed their anger and disapproval of the law by way of a strongly worded letter.

Laws forbidding common use of a facility by both white persons and Negroes are often thought to come primarily from the Plessy v. Ferguson decision. The essential contribution of the Plessy case was its sanction of state classification of citizens on a racial basis. But there was nothing in that case that stated Negroes could be wholly excluded by law from use of a facility open to the public. The Plessy case stated that segregation was approved on the theory that the constitutional command for equal protection of the law was satisfied when separate and equal facilities were provided for Negroes.

In the Berea case, however, not only was racial classification approved by the state but the state was permitted to command overt racial discrimination by ordering exclusion of a Negro from a place to which he had been extended a welcome. Neither the state nor any private individual was under any duty to provide separate facilities, equal, or even comparable, to those from which he had been excluded because of race.

It was obvious that the states rightists had a clear and Supreme Court-sanctioned mandate to enforce segregation as the law of the land. What had been a flood of discrimination that overflowed the walls of justice and decency, increased to a raging torrent once those walls collapsed. This was so in public transportation, in the schools, in the courts, and in every aspect of the inevitable interracial conflicts that ensued. And little or no change was in sight for years to come. Into the 1950s racial segregation continued to permeate all aspects of life in the south.

After the Berea decision, city and state legislators became increasingly creative in fashioning laws to deny blacks their constitutional rights. It was in 1906, that Montgomery passed a law authorizing separate streetcars.

In 1951, the Rev. Vernon Johns, then minister of Montgomery's Dexter Avenue Baptist Church had tried to prompt a group of blacks to leave the bus in protest of patent mistreatment. He stood up and challenged the other blacks to march off the bus with him. They told him they weren't moving. "You ought to know better," one said.[8]

In 1953, the black community in Baton Rouge, Louisiana, successfully petitioned the city council to pass an ordinance allowing blacks to be seated on a first-come, first-serve basis on city buses. Blacks would still have to begin their seating at the back of the bus while whites would sit up front; but no seats were to be actually reserved for whites.

The white Baton Rouge bus drivers, however, ignored the ordinance and continued to save seats for whites. In an effort to demand compliance with the new ordinance, the black community staged a bus boycott. But by day's end, the Louisiana attorney general declared the new ordinance illegal and ruled that the drivers did not have to change the seating practices on the buses. The strike ended unsuccessfully.

Three months later, blacks in Baton Rouge again launched a bus boycott. This action lasted only about a week. Yet, city officials were induced to offer a compromise regarding the seating, and blacks accepted it. This boycott marked one of the first times a community of blacks had organized a sustained action against segregation and won, albeit, a small victory. Although the success in Baton Rouge was overshadowed by the landmark 1954 Supreme Court decision regarding school desegregation, the lessons learned were germane and lasting.[9]

Pending before the United States Supreme Court in 1952, were cases from the states of Kansas, South Carolina, Virginia and Delaware. Each was premised on different facts and different local conditions, but a common legal question justified their consideration together in a consolidated opinion. In each of the cases, Negro minors sought the aid of the Court in obtaining admission to the public schools of their community on a non-segregated basis. In each instance, they had been denied admission to schools attended by white children under laws requiring or permitting segregation according to race. The segregation was alleged to deprive plaintiffs of the equal protection of the laws under the Fourteenth Amendment.

The name of Oliver Brown was selected from the alphabetical listing of all petitioners and the consolidated case was therein known as Brown v. Board of Education of Topeka.[10] Brown had filed the suit against Kansas on behalf of his eight year old daughter. In the Brown v Board of Education of Topeka and the companion cases, the question of separate but equal was directly presented. The Court was called upon to determine if segregation in public schools deprived these plaintiffs of equal protection of the laws. Or, more specifically, the question was, "Does segregation of children in public schools solely on the basis of race, even though the physical facilities and other 'tangible' factors may be equal, deprive the children of the minority group, equal educational opportunities?"

Thurgood Marshall, then a NAACP lawyer, argued the case for the plaintiffs. The Court's opinion, written by Chief Justice Earl Warren who persuaded the dissenters to his side for an unanimous decision, concluded that in the field of public education, the doctrine separate but equal, has no place. The

Court said separate educational facilities are inherently unequal. We hold that the plaintiffs and others, similarly situated, for whom the actions have been brought are, by reason of the segregation complained of, deprived of the equal protection of the laws guaranteed by the Fourteenth Amendment. This landmark decision, chipping away at the citadel of bigotry, was delivered on Monday, May 17, 1954. This was only a beginning.

However, in spite of or in some instances, because of the favorable ruling in the 1954 Brown case, hatred and bigotry ran rampant and numerous lives were lost. Persons were murdered for little or no reason during the years that followed. The Emmett Till case serves to reflect the mood of the time.

Emmett Louis Till was fourteen years old when he left Chicago, in the summer of 1955, to spend time with his cousins in Money, Mississippi. Unaware of the harsh etiquette that governed race relations in Mississippi, Till, acting on a dare from his cousins, said "Bye, Baby" to Carolyn Bryant, a white cashier in a country store where he had bought some candy. Soon, almost everyone in Money had heard some version of the story: A black boy had "sassed" a white woman.

Later that night, Bryant's husband, James, and his half brother, J.W. Milam, went looking for "the boy that did the talking." They found Emmett at the home of his great uncle, Mose Wright, and took him away. Days later, a white teenager out fishing, found Emmett's body floating in the Tallahatchie River.

Milam, later, told a magazine writer that he and Bryant beat Emmett, shot him in the head, wired a cotton gin fan to his neck, and dumped him into the river. When asked why he had done it, Milam shrugged nonchalantly, and replied, "Well, what else could I do? He thought he was as good as any white man." Emmett's bereaved mother, Mamie Till, journeyed to Mississippi, and insisted on taking her son's body back home with her. In

Chicago, she arranged an open-casket funeral so that all the world could see what had been done to her son, Emmett. One eye was gouged out, and his head was crushed on one side. Thousands attended the funeral. Whites in Mississippi raised $10,000 to cover the legal costs of the accused, Bryant and Milam. Emmett's uncle, Mose Wright, in an extraordinary act of courage, rose in the crowded court room to point out Bryant and Milam as the men who took Emmett Till away. The brothers admitted they had kidnapped and beaten Emmett but claimed they left him alive. It took the all-white jury only a little over an hour to return a verdict of not guilty.[11]

Many historians allow the martyrdom of Emmett Till to overshadow those who might properly be viewed as the outstanding heroes of this senseless tragedy. Till never understood the danger he innocently mocked. It was the deliberate actions of his mother and uncle that gave meaning to the sacrifice of Emmett to the idol of white supremacy.

Thanks to his mother and uncle, Emmett's murder was transfigured into a national event that gave impetus to the growing sense of outrage that many felt towards the jim crow regime. Mamie Till spoke out about her son's death and forced the country to recognize the horror of lynching.

After Mose Wright testified against his nephew's murderers, he was driven from his home by vengeful, racist whites. One of the people who helped him to escape from Mississippi was Medgar Evers, a young activist who had just become the state's first NAACP field secretary.[12]

TWO

The Bus Ride

Thusly, on December 1, 1955, Rosa Parks, as did Homer Plessy sixty-three years before, refused to budge from her seat. The police were called, and they came to the scene and arrested her.

News reports of this confrontation erroneously emphasized that Mrs. Parks' fatigue from a hard day's work propelled her into history, not heroism. She was fully aware, through her work with the NAACP, of the many cases where black passengers were "insulted, whipped, brutally beaten and even shot," by police or their surrogates, the bus drivers. Mrs. Parks recalled many instances where black women were insulted, roughed up, and physically assaulted on city buses.[1]

Of all her memories of such assaults, one in which the NAACP was involved, was the most painful to recall. An infirm black male, still under the doctor's care, boarded a bus enroute home. He and the hefty driver came to a hasty disagreement and exchanged a few unpleasantries. The passenger got off at his stop and was still there when the bus driver returned. The driver stopped the bus, disengaged the bus coin changer, and crossed the street. Using the coin changer as a brass knuckle, "He beat the poor man unmercifully." The case came to court and the passenger, not the driver, was found guilty.

These and other memories disturbed Mrs. Parks as she waited for the police to arrive. "I was well aware of what could happen or what might happen to me, other than just being arrested," she later recalled. Despite the threats, Mrs. Parks kept her cool and she kept her seat.

At this crucial moment, Rosa Parks made an important personal decision. She opted for her personal dignity and human freedom. She decided to resist; in doing so, she took on the bus driver, the law, and the entire racial system that for years had oppressed and degraded her and her people.

The bus driver returned, reinforced with two burly white policemen, who asked Mrs. Parks if the driver had requested her to move. She said, "Yes." One policeman, unable to understand such obstinacy, wanted to know why she would not vacate the seat. Mrs. Parks replied that she did not think she should have to stand up so someone else could have her seat. Continuing to speak to the policeman, she asked, "Why do you always push us around?" Sincerely, she wanted to know why the police and bus officials continued to abuse and take advantage of Negroes. The officer said he did not know and placed her under arrest.

The officers picked up Mrs. Parks' belongings and escorted her to their patrol car and on to city hall. She was charged with violating Chapter 6, Section 11 of the City Code.

The policy of the Montgomery City Lines bus company was written in keeping with city and state ordinances on segregation. Drivers were to designate the front part of the bus for whites and the rear section for blacks in proportion to the number of blacks and whites on the bus at any given moment. As more whites came onto the bus, the driver moved an imaginary color line further to the rear of the bus. Blacks, sitting directly behind the 'whites-only' section, would be ordered to move further toward the rear of the bus, if whites had to stand.

The official policy, theoretically, was that if there were no vacant seats available behind the imaginary color line, blacks did not have to stand for whites to sit. But, in practice, whenever a white person had to stand, the driver would look in the rear view mirror and yell at the 'Nigras' to move to the back of the bus, even if there were no vacant seats.

The police transported Mrs. Parks to the city jail where she was fingerprinted, photographed and booked as a common criminal. In due course, she was allowed one telephone call. Her mother answered the phone. When Rosa told her where she was, fearing the worst, her mother screamed, "Did they beat you?" Mrs. Parks assured her mother that she was, "all right," briefly explaining what had happened, and she asked to have her husband come and get her out of jail.[2]

Raymond Parks immediately called Charlie Newsome, a white friend, and told him what had happened and asked for his help. Newsome explained he was ready for bed, but Parks told him to put his clothes back on. "I want you to go and stand her bond!" Parks told him he'd be there in three minutes and he started right out the back door. "I was real excited," he said.[3]

After the phone call, Mrs. Parks was returned to her cell, already occupied by two other women. While sitting in jail waiting for her family, Rosa became much distressed and angry over what had happened. She later confided that, "I wasn't happy at all; I don't recall being extremely frightened, but I felt very much annoyed and inconvenienced because I had hoped to go home and get my dinner, and do whatever else I had to do for the evening. But now here I was sitting in jail and couldn't get home."

Because Rosa L. Parks is an essential figure in this story, an insight into her background and character is provided. Rosa L. McCauley was born February 4, 1913, in Tuskegee, Alabama. Her father, James McCauley was a carpenter, and her mother, Leona, had once been a teacher. While still a little girl, the McCauley family moved to a little farm on the outskirts of Montgomery, Alabama.

Rosa first attended a small, one-room school in Pine Level, rural, Montgomery county, which had shutters for windows. Lighting was provided by the sun shining through openings in the walls. Not too far from where she lived was a new school for whites. The white students had buses to take them back and forth to school. The black students were afforded no such luxury. Rosa Parks, reflecting on her childhood, once recalled, "I'd see the bus pass my house every day. But to me, that was a way of life; we had no choice but to accept what was the custom." She went on to comment, "The bus was among the first ways I realized there was a black world and a white world."[4]

Later, Rosa attended the Montgomery Industrial School for Girls, better known as Miss White's School. This school was established during the Reconstruction period by the American Missionary Association and staffed mainly by white, New England, female teachers. They journeyed South every year to open the school from late fall through spring, to teach the Colored women. Because Montgomery had no public elementary school in these early years, Miss White's school served that purpose and offered courses up to the eighth grade.

Aside from giving the Negro pupils a very sound academic foundation, Miss White's school instructed them in personal hygiene, how to cook, sew, and keep house, in short, to be good homemakers. The education offered there was grounded in Christian values. Chapel service was held every Friday morning, where singing and prayers dominated the service.

Those who attended the Congregational school were taught to live by the Golden Rule, "to do unto others as you would have them do unto you, that honesty was the best policy, that they had a personal worth and that they had an obligation to themselves, their family and the community to be useful contributing citizens."[5]

Young Rosa grew up in a difficult environment. As a child, she heard of the Ku Klux Klan and its lawless oppression of blacks. She had heard of black people's homes being burned and their schools leveled to the ground. The stories of her people being beaten, dragged from their homes and killed, and lynchings were frequently brought to her attention. She grew up in this atmosphere of lawlessness, where barbarism flourished, where white people could terrorize black people with impunity, and where her family and others like it were constantly under threat.

Rosa Parks remembered that her grandfather always kept an old shotgun close by, but she wondered how effective he would have been with it if serious trouble did come their way. She somehow was able to escape hostility toward white people generally, despite the prevailing atmosphere. But she had little trouble understanding that the Ku Klux Klan was the "enemy." Her family often discussed the severe conditions under which they lived. "The upper most subject," she vividly recalled, "would not be integration and enjoying the same opportunities and accommodations as white people, but survival and avoiding trouble with white people."

Her's was a church-going family, members of the African Methodist Episcopal Church. Mrs. Parks recalled that, "All we ever heard about was the hereafter and heaven — spirituals on how when I get there, I'm going to put on my shoes and shout all over God's heaven. I guess it must have grown out of the times when slaves who went without shoes and proper clothing could think that while deprived here, there would be a heaven after death where they could enjoy all the wonderful things they didn't have on earth."

Mrs. Parks learned about slavery, and what it meant to be legally considered the property of others with all its accompanying abuses, from her maternal grandparents, both of whom had been born into slavery. "My grandmother," she remembered, "told how where she was, there were never any provisions for feeding the slave children except from a huge pot in the yard, where they poured it into a trough like feeding pigs or chickens."

Her grandfather, the son of a slave owner, "was thrown out and treated very badly when his father died. Early in life, he became a cripple, went without shoes and the proper clothing in the winter and was severely beaten by the overseer."[6]

Due to the strength of character of her family and, particularly, the sense of self-respect and counsel always to be proud of herself instilled by her mother, Rosa developed a healthy self-concept and cultivated a deep and abiding respect for black people. Her mother, as one writer discovered, "taught her not to judge people by the amount of money that they had, nor the kind of houses they lived in, nor the clothes they wore. People should be judged by the respect they have for themselves and others." These values and ideas, no doubt, influenced Mrs. Parks' thinking and helped to prepare her to meet the challenges she would face later in life.[7]

Rosa McCauley continued her education and later worked at a variety of local jobs. She developed into a hardworking and industrious woman. On December 18, 1932, she married Raymond Parks, a barber. At that time, he was involved in fund raising efforts to defend the Scottsboro Boys, in one of Alabama's most shameful and longest trials.

Concerned about the difficulties Negroes faced in living under the oppressive system of racial segregation and wanting to do something to change that condition, Mrs. Parks joined the local NAACP and began working as its branch secretary, a job she held for nearly twelve years. E.D. Nixon was president of the local chapter during those years. He found Mrs. Parks to be a responsible, dutiful worker who gave generously of her time and energy, furthering the direction of the organization. She frequently assisted with voter registration drives to get more blacks the franchise.

When the U.S. Supreme Court ruled against segregation in 1954, she, and others in the community, were elated. "I felt," she said, "that there might be still more possibility of not having to continue as we had." Volunteer work in the church and in the community and her employment at the NAACP helped to prepare Mrs. Parks for her future role in the Civil Rights Movement.

One summer, Rosa Parks attended an extended seminar at Myles Horton's Highlander Folk School in Tennessee, the first time that she had lived in an integrated environment. Virginia Durr, a white friend and the wife of liberal attorney Clifford Durr, urged Rosa to attend the school. No doubt the social and educational benefits of this experience influenced her thinking considerably in regard to race relations. Coming a few months before the Montgomery Bus Boycott, the training was most opportune.

Highlander Folk School was established in 1932, in Monteagle, Tennessee, by Myles Horton, a teacher and community activist. The problems of oppressed workers, in the Appalachian Mountains, were the initial items on Highlander's agenda. The school offered workshops on labor unions, workers' rights and recreation. During the 1950s and 1960s, however, the school evolved into a training ground for civil rights activists. Horton concentrated on identifying new leaders, training and sending them out into the field to continue their education and their involvement in civil rights.

Horton also had a successful program in which black adults were taught to read and write and, thereby, qualify to vote. The first teacher of this program was Bernice Robinson, a hairdresser. Sessions were held two nights a week in the rear of a small store. Horton did not want the classes to be run as a regular school, with the usual routine by a trained teacher. Robinson taught the students what they wanted to learn: how to write their names, letters and how to cash checks.

Not surprisingly, Highlander faced stiff opposition from white segregationists. In 1957, the IRS revoked the school's tax-exempt status. In 1959, Arkansas attorney general, Bruce Bennett, initiated a hearing to determine if the Highlander School was part of a communist conspiracy. In 1960, the school's charter was revoked. Horton was found guilty of selling beer without a license and of violating a Tennessee law that forbade blacks and whites from attending school together, despite the 1954, Brown ruling of the U.S. Supreme Court. Horton fought back and Highlander withstood the attack.

Horton first moved his school to Knoxville and, later, to New Market, Tennessee. Rosa received her final certification as a freedom fighter from the school, joining the ranks of other civil rights alumni as John Lewis, James Bevel, and Martin Luther King, Jr.[8]

Reflecting on those formative years, Mrs. Parks admitted, "All this took a good part of my life. It was a struggle − I don't know if you would call it that − just to be human, to be a citizen, to have the rights and privileges of any other person."

Thus, this Negro seamstress, on the eve of her heroic act of civil disobedience, which became a direct challenge to the status quo, was deeply committed to the welfare of black people in Montgomery and to the principles of racial justice.

At the time of Rosa's arrest, another rider who witnessed the incident, left the bus and ran to the home of Bertha Butler, a friend and co-worker of Mrs. Parks and told her of the arrest. Mrs. Butler then ran several blocks to E.D. Nixon's house for help.[9] It is interesting to note, as Mrs. Parks would later comment, "Mrs. Butler went to the Nixon home, because Mr. Nixon was the person people usually called on when they were in trouble."

Mr. Nixon was not home, and Mrs. Butler told his wife, Arlet, about the arrest. Mrs. Nixon called her husband's office and left a message for him to call home as soon as possible.

Over the years, Nixon had taken the lead in many civil rights causes. He organized the Montgomery Welfare League, the Montgomery Voters League, Boy Scout Troops, senior citizen activities, and ran for a spot on the Montgomery County Democratic Executive Committee. Nixon was former head of the

NAACP, the local as well as the Alabama state chapter.

Nixon had worked for many years, as a sleeping car porter, mainly on the Montgomery to Chicago run. He worked closely with A. Philip Randolph and helped organize the Brotherhood of Sleeping Car Porters. He served as local president of the Union.

Mrs. Johnnie Carr, praising E.D. Nixon and describing some of the problems confronting the Montgomery community in earlier times, recalled a situation concerning Oak Park, a large park area, bordering her home. The city, using it as a dumping ground and storage area for manure, would intermittently return and load trucks with manure to deposit around the city as fertilizer for plants. The park area became infested with flies to the point that residents could not sit on their porches or in their yards. Neighborhood people had exhausted all efforts to force the city to refrain from the dumping and storage of manure, but to no avail.

One morning, Mrs. Carr was standing in her kitchen, crying, disgusted with the swarms of flies in and around her house. She decided to call E.D. Nixon. His immediate reaction was, "Sue the city. Collect one hundred dollars so that you can file the suit," and he recommended white attorneys Azar and Campbell. The attorneys were at the park the next day, with cameras. Eventually, the suit was successful and the park was cleared. This was in the 1940s, but Montgomery's citizens can relate many such stories of similar incidents when Nixon came to the rescue throughout the years.[10]

So it is understandable why Bertha Butler sought him out. When Nixon returned to his office, he called his wife who blurted, "They arrested Mrs. Parks!" She urged her husband to, "Go get her!" Nixon immediately called police headquarters and asked why Mrs. Parks had been arrested and what charges were being brought against her?

The white officer, another guardian of the status quo, retorted that it was, "None of your damn business."

Attorney Fred Gray, who had handled cases for NAACP, was out of town; so Nixon called Attorney Clifford Durr and asked him to call the police station and find out what the charges were against Mrs. Parks. Durr secured the information and informed Nixon that Mrs. Parks was charged with violating the Alabama bus segregation law.

Nixon told Durr that he was going to the city jail and post bond for her. Durr offered to come along. Virginia Durr, Clifford's wife, accompanied them. She and Rosa had established a strong bond of friendship over a period of several years.[11]

Nixon and the Durrs reached the jail before Mr. Parks and Mr. Newsome arrived. The desk officer started to hand the bond papers, releasing Mrs. Parks, to Clifford Durr. Durr halted the officer and said, "No, Mr. Nixon is the property owner, he is going to sign." The bond was one hundred dollars. The officer then handed the papers to Nixon who signed them.

This first act of securing Mrs. Parks' release went against a tradition that was older than the Republic, itself. Never was a black man's signature to be accepted if a white man's was available. Although Nixon had assisted other blacks in trouble, even by signing small bonds, these cases were insignificant to the police. This time, the police realized that this was a more serious situation and chose, from the outset, to ignore Nixon.

In the past, the Negro was not expected to know how to sign his name. All that was considered possible for him was to make an "X" and have it countersigned by a white person. Certainly, Durr's deliberate act of passing the release form to Nixon for his signature did not win him any friends at city hall. Even from the beginning, this case was to be different.

The officer asked Nixon what day did he want Mrs. Parks' case to be heard. Saturday or Monday were the choices. Nixon, scheduled to go out of town over the weekend, chose Monday morning. He conferred with Durr who assured him that Fred Gray would have returned by that time.

All matters settled, the police released Mrs. Parks from jail. Upon seeing her, Virginia Durr embraced Mrs. Parks "down there in the presence of all those white people." Nixon and Durr felt a sigh of relief. Within a moment Mrs. Parks' husband and Mr. Newsome arrived. The entourage, except Newsome, accompanied Mrs. Parks home.

That night in her apartment, Mrs. Parks retold what had happened on the bus. As her mother served everyone coffee, E.D. Nixon suggested that this was the case they needed to challenge the legality of the bus practice and demonstrate their anger at the treatment they had received. Nixon added, "if we could just get all the Negroes to stay off the bus one day, just to show the bus company where the money comes from, that would be an important demonstration. We can boycott the bus lines with this and at the same time go to the Supreme Court," Nixon suggested.

Nixon asked Mrs. Parks to give him her permission to use her bus incident as a case to test the constitutionality of the local city bus ordinance. Nixon said he would work to rally community support around Mrs. Parks and call for a day of protest, Monday, December 5th. Everybody would stay off the buses to show their disapproval of what had happened to her and the existing bus conditions. He knew, as he revealed later, "If Mrs. Parks says yes, hell could freeze, but she wouldn't change. And she was intelligent enough to take care of herself in court." But when Nixon first put the question to her, she was unsure about committing herself and said she did not know.[12]

Few could deny that the bus situation had been a serious problem for many, many years. As head of the NAACP for some of those years, E.D. Nixon had fought the problem and had tried to get a test case to challenge the legality of the city bus code.

This was consistent with his overall fight against segregation and racial discrimination throughout the city.

One observer of the Montgomery scene noted that most of the black bus riders on any particular day were women. Men tended to avoid the embarrassment of confrontation by walking, hitchhiking and arranging rides. Certainly, this method of travel was more convenient for men than for women. Consequently, all of the litigants who challenged the racist system, in the courts, were women.

Nixon remembered the bus incident, long ago, when Reverend Wingfield's daughter, Katie, was arrested and he refused to get involved in the case. Considering the attitude of the girl's father, Nixon believed that her case would not get very far. Commenting on Wingfield, Nixon said, "He was one of those who believes in what the white folk say."

In 1944, Nixon took up the case of Viola White, another woman who had been arrested on the bus, badly beaten, and jailed. He hired a lawyer, but the local court found her guilty and fined her ten dollars plus court costs. He appealed the case, but waited year after year for the officials to have it put on the court docket. Over ten years passed. The woman died, and "her case never was heard."

Nixon was active when Claudette Colvin was arrested. She was a fifteen-year old student who was seated near the rear of the bus. All seats were eventually taken, and the aisle was crowded. The bus driver ordered all blacks to stand; all the black men left the bus. Colvin refused to get up. The driver became enraged, drove the bus non-stop to town and summoned the police. The police dragged her, kicking and screaming hysterically, off the bus and drove her to jail.

Two carloads of people converged on Nixon's house to help plan a strategy for what could be done, including Jo Ann Robinson, Dr. Mary Fair Burks, and James Pierce. They thought they had the test case they had been looking for and a victim around whom community support could be rallied for a general protest. Few would attempt a boycott without Nixon being a part of it; therefore, conferring with him was essential.

Nixon interviewed Claudette Colvin and her parents and was convinced that she would not serve as a good litigant around whom to marshall community opposition to the buses. Remembering the occasion, Nixon recalled, "Jo Ann Robinson liked to have had a fit. She jumped all over me." Nixon stuck to his appraisal of the situation saying, "She's not the kind we can win a case with."

In October 1955, Mary Louise Smith, 18 years of age, was arrested and fined for refusing to move to the rear of the bus. Nixon appraised the case; but, once again, he thought the victim was inappropriate. To their disappointment, Nixon, also, ruled her out for the lack of "proper" community symbol.[13]

With Mrs. Parks, however, Nixon believed he had an even better case than he could have hoped for. She had a good, clean-cut reputation, one of service and kindness to those in need.

A long time resident of Montgomery, Rosa Parks was warmly regarded and highly respected in the black community. Unpleasant experiences on the buses were common to her as with many black people. "How ironic," Nixon admitted years later. "We hadn't planned on Mrs. Parks being a test case. We just stumbled onto it when she was arrested."

There were others who recognized the luck in having a person like Rosa Parks symbolize the evil of racial segregation in public transportation. L.D. Reddick, an Alabama State College professor, described Mrs. Parks as an "attractive Negro woman who was ideally fitted for her role. A member of St. Pauls AME Church, this avid church-goer looked like the symbol of Mother's Day."[14] To Reverend Edgar N. French, another asset was that she was not a member of the rich upper or well-to-do middle classes but a typical, American housewife who shared in the support of her household by working. "What was important was the character of this woman who was held in high esteem by her fellow parishioners," recalled French. "Although mild-mannered and soft-spoken, the warmth and radiance of her personality bespoke her presence in almost any setting."[15]

James E. Pierce remembered Mrs. Parks as a "quiet, unassuming, Christian lady with a great deal of civic concern and community interest." Furthermore, Pierce commented that this "Christian leader" was a "devout member of the NAACP, and she knew what these people were doing to break down this segregation."[16]

Nevertheless, Mrs. Parks remained undecided. She needed time to discuss the matter with her husband and mother. In such a closely built family as hers, they would have a role to play if she agreed to join in the project.

She presented the issues to them. Raymond, concerned about his wife's welfare, was hesitant about giving his approval. Mrs. McCauley left the matter up to them, agreeing to support their decision. Their discussion continued for some time after the others left. Finally, Mr. and Mrs. Parks agreed that she would join the struggle and lend her name to the effort to integrate the public transportation system.

She conveyed their decision to Mr. Nixon, "If you think we can get anywhere with it, I'll go along with it."[17] Nixon expressed his appreciation and went on to complete what was to become a team of great resilience and responsibility for the proposed project.

THREE

Community Response

With Rosa's cooperation assured, Nixon moved quickly through the morning of the second of December to put his team together before leaving town that afternoon. Attorney Gray had served well with Attorney Charles D. Langford's help on several civil right cases for the NAACP. The two lawyers, fearless and aggressive, had won the respect of their colleagues and the judges before whom they appeared. While it may never be needed, Nixon was assured to know that the legal counsel of the more experienced attorney Durr, was available at a moment's call. Crucial to the execution of the one-day bus boycott proposed for December 5th, three days hence, was the urgent need to get the word out to the black community. Nixon realized that there was more involved than a protest against the arrest of Mrs. Parks. There was a greater need to mount a general protest against racial segregation in public transportation. Since nearly every one was victimized by the system, he wanted to mobilize the total community in support of this statement of outrage. As is true in most black communities, the best method of reaching vast numbers of citizens is through the churches. Nixon's long experience as community leader and head of the NAACP in prior years, had brought him into a cooperative relationship with many of the leaders of the black community. With the few hours left before departure, he had to move decisively. He would return too late, on Sunday, to implement a Monday boycott. Nixon drew from the resources, accumulated over the years, to mobilize the community.

The first of his many calls was to Reverend Ralph Abernathy, pastor of the First Baptist Church. It had one of the largest black congregations in the city and was one of the oldest churches. He knew that if he was successful in enlisting Abernathy's aid, the other black ministers would encourage their members to support the proposed boycott. Abernathy was a young, dynamic preacher who was well known and highly respected for his unwavering commitment to work for social advancement of black people.

Tactically, Nixon recognized his limitations in not knowing personally all the ministers in town. Furthermore, he realized that even if he had known all of them, he questioned whether he could get them to be totally committed to his campaign on the strength of his argument and personality alone. He did believe, however, that if he got the cooperation of most of the leading ministers with large congregations who were progressive in their thinking, he could sway the rest.

Nixon told Abernathy what had happened to Mrs. Parks and that he believed that here was a case that possibly could be used to "test" the bus company. Furthermore, he reminded the preacher that Mrs. Parks was, "the kind of woman that'll stand up." Abernathy agreed wholeheartedly that there should be a boycott, saying, "Let me know what you want me to do and tell me what anybody else says." Nixon asked Abernathy to call a meeting of black ministers, in order to, "organize the boycott."

Nixon, next called Reverend H.H. Hubbard, pastor of the Bethel Baptist Church, who had often come to the aid of victimized and needy blacks. Hubbard, Nixon's pastor, was a man of age and maturity, in whom the Pullman porter had profound faith and trust. Nixon knew, "he'd go along." Rev. Hubbard confirmed that judgement, saying simply without hesitation, "Yes, I'll go along."[1]

Nixon's third call was to Reverend Martin Luther King, Jr., the recently-appointed pastor of Dexter Avenue Baptist Church.

Nixon, again, explained what had happened to Mrs. Parks. King listened and was, "deeply shocked" upon hearing of another affront to a decent black citizen. Nixon told King that, "We have taken this type of thing too long, already... I feel that the time has come to boycott the buses. Only through a boycott can we make it clear to the white folks that we will not accept this type of treatment any longer." King needed time to consider the proposal.

Sometime later, Nixon called King, again, and secured a firmer commitment of his support. King volunteered the use of his church as a site to hold an organizational meeting that evening.

In the meantime, Reverend Abernathy, fully committed to the campaign, had begun to contact others. He had participated in all of the meetings with city and bus officials over the previous two years. He knew that the white authorities had promised to solve the bus problems but had done nothing. "We must do it ourselves."

At that time, Abernathy served as secretary of the Baptist Ministerial Alliance, which facilitated his reaching all the other black Baptist leaders in town. He, too, called Reverend H.H. Hubbard, who was president of the Baptist Ministerial Alliance.

After talking with Abernathy, Hubbard called a meeting of all the conference's pastors. The senior minister often relied on Abernathy to organize meetings and initiate programs for the conference. By calling a meeting in the name of the president, they felt a large number of ministers would come, thinking that the call was for a session of the Baptist Conference.[2]

Within hours, Abernathy got word to all the Baptist ministers. He then thought it would be a good idea to get the Methodist and AME Zion ministers involved. After a few calls, he learned that the AME Zion ministers were holding a conference that day with their Bishop in Hilliard Chapel, Reverend Edgar N. French's church. Abernathy went to the church and spoke with Reverend

L. Roy Bennett, who, unprecedentedly, interceded with the Bishop and got permission for Abernathy to speak to the AME Zion group.

Abernathy told the AME Zion ministers that Mrs. Parks had been arrested; and, because of the concern of a number of citizens, a group of preachers had decided to deal with the matter in an emergency meeting at Dexter Avenue Baptist Church that night. Abernathy asked the preachers to come to the meeting. Reverend Bennett and the others, "outraged" over what had happened to Mrs. Parks, agreed to cooperate in every way they could, and practically all of them promised to come to the meeting that night.[3]

Throughout the morning hours, the three men, Nixon, Abernathy and King, worked diligently to encourage all the community leaders to attend the meeting. Nixon continued his calls until it was time to catch his train for Chicago.

The limitations imposed by his job, as Pullman porter, did not prevent Nixon from active involvement in all segments of the community. Moving beyond the ministers, Nixon called history professor, James E. Pierce of Alabama State College, and one or two officers of the well-motivated and highly-organized, Women's Political Council (WPC).[4] Despite his job and a fourth grade education, Nixon had earned wide respect and was accepted as a leader by all segments of the black community.

Although the ministers made these calls on Friday morning, urging attendance at the evening meeting to discuss the possibility of calling for a bus boycott for the following Monday, the boycott was already in motion. Jo Ann Gibson Robinson, an English professor at Alabama State College, tells in her book, *The Montgomery Bus Boycott and the Women Who Started It,*[5] of the drama that began almost immediately after the arrest of Rosa Parks.

Thursday night, when Attorney Gray returned to the city and responded to Robinson's request that he return her call, she related what she had heard about Mrs. Parks' arrest. Gray and his wife, Bernice, were close friends of Robinson. They knew that Robinson and other members of the WPC had been, for many months, preparing for a bus boycott and only awaited the proper moment for its execution. Robinson agreed that this was the appropriate time. Gray gave Robinson encouragement and his blessing to proceed with the plan. She described her next move, "I sat down and quickly drafted a message and then called a good friend and colleague, John Cannon, chairman of the business department at Alabama State College, who had access to the College's mimeograph equipment. Along with two of my trusted senior students, we quickly agreed to meet almost immediately in the middle of the night at the College's duplicating room. We were able to get three messages to a mimeograph page. By four o'clock in the morning, sheets had been duplicated, cut in thirds and bundled."

The mimeographed message read as follows:

This is for Monday, December 5, 1955. Another Negro woman has been arrested and thrown into jail because she refused to get up out of her seat on the bus for a white person to sit down. It is the second time since the Claudette Colvin case that a Negro woman had been arrested for the same thing. This has to be stopped. Negroes have rights, too, for if Negroes did not ride the buses, they could not operate. Three-fourths of the riders are Negroes, yet we are arrested, or have to stand behind empty seats. If you do not do something to stop those arrests, they will continue. The next time it may be you, or your daughter or your mother.

This woman's case will come up on Monday. We are, therefore, asking every Negro to stay off the buses Monday in protest of the arrest and trial. Don't ride the buses to work, to town, to school, or anywhere on Monday. You can afford to stay out of school for one day if you have no other way to go except by bus. You also can afford to stay out of town for one day. If you work, take a cab or walk. But please, children and grownups, don't ride the bus at all on Monday. Please stay off of all buses, Monday.

From 4 :00 a.m. to 7:00 a.m., Mrs Robinson and the students mapped out routes where the leaflets would be distributed. WPC members, mobilized by the early call, arranged to help with the distribution, by waiting at certain planned drop-off points.

"Later that day," writes Mrs. Robinson, "when H. Councill Trenholm, the president of Alabama State College, got wind of what had happened, I was summoned into his office." She admitted using 35 reams of paper (at 500 sheets/ream), between midnight and dawn. They had made 17,000 sheets, cut in thirds, for a total of 52,500 leaflets, for which Mrs. Robinson was requested to pay, and did.

Alabama State College, with a faculty of almost 200 and a student body of about 2,000, was the largest institution of higher learning in Montgomery, and the cultural center of Montgomery's black community. Considerable controversy resulted from the fact that the College's faculty and facilities played a significant role in the success of the Montgomery Bus Boycott.

A review of Alabama State College's history discloses that controversy has been a regular companion since it was founded in the Lincoln School in Marion, Alabama, soon after the Civil War. Due to the number of schools for teaching white students, Marion was called the "Athens of the South." For black students, the story was just the opposite.

Freedmen wanted to educate their children, also, but without the influence and assistance of their former masters, whom they did not trust. On July 17, 1867, nine black men met, organized and incorporated the Lincoln School (named for Abraham

Lincoln) of Marion, Alabama. Of these nine men, only two could sign their names on the incorporation papers. The group bought a small plot of land and started to build a schoolhouse, but ran out of funds.

The American Missionary Association (AMA) and the Freedmen's Bureau came to their assistance. When built, the school was leased to the AMA, who furnished teachers, books and administrative know-how.

Through the influence of the AMA and the school officials, one of whom, Alexander Curtis, was a member of the Alabama State Senate, the state of Alabama was encouraged to establish a Normal, teacher-training, school at Lincoln. Under the authority of the state assembly, the Enabling Act was approved on December 2, 1869, with a start-up appropriation of $2,000. Thus, the first school in the United States supported by state funds to train black teachers was begun, and, eventually became Alabama State College.

Unhappy members of the white community burned down the school in 1887, and insisted that it not be rebuilt. Reaching a compromise, the State General Assembly abolished Lincoln's, Normal school segment, named it Alabama Colored People's University and began a search for a new site.

By an act of the Assembly, an appropriation of $10,000 was allocated for a building and $7,500 a year for the operation of the university. The act provided for a Board of Trustees, of which Governor Seay was ex-officio president and Superintendent Palmer, a member ex-officio was chosen to manage its affairs. After considering several sites, the school was finally transferred to Montgomery.

Montgomery's black citizens pledged and raised $5,000 in money and land for the use of the University to show their appreciation for the location in their city. The president of the Assembly was authorized to rent temporary quarters until the building, provided for in the Act, could be erected. The school opened on October 3, 1887, in a church building six years after Booker T. Washington came to nearby Tuskegee to establish the Tuskegee Normal and Industrial Institute.

Controversy began immediately. The constitutionality of the Enabling Act was contested in the courts, finally reaching the State Supreme Court. The decision, rendered the following April, held: "that the 7th and 10th sections of the act are unconstitutional and as what remains is incapable of full execution according to legislative intent, the entire Act fails."

The decision was based upon the assumption that the appropriation for common schools could not be used to build a university. The effect of this decision was to prevent the further use of the money appropriated in the Act, but it did revive the State Normal school at Marion. But rather than face the anger of Marion's white citizens, it was deemed less hazardous to remain in Montgomery until the next session of the General Assembly, when definite action could be taken.

Meanwhile, additional opposition arose from two other sources. There was a general white hostility within the state legislature against any school for blacks, especially for higher education. Some legislators suggested a tax be levied against Tuskegee on the land that had been granted for establishing that school. When it was pointed out that such a levy would require a similar charge against the larger holdings of the University of Alabama in Tuscaloosa, opposition ceased.

Booker T. Washington was not pleased that another school was to be located so close to Tuskegee. It was pointed out that the new school was primarily for the training of teachers and would in no way compete with the industrial and agricultural emphasis of Tuskegee. Washington countered that Tuskegee had a Normal school and was, already beginning to train and recruit teachers for schools in Alabama's Black Belt, the area of greatest need.

The trustees and officers were able to survive these and other impediments and the school's second section was opened in September 1888, with an attendance of 250, which by the middle of November, following, was increased to 500. The first installment of $2,500 was drawn before measures were begun to test the constitutionality of the Act. School officials received $500.00 from the Peabody Fund with which, by the aid of voluntary contributions by Colored people, they were able to carry on the school through the school year but incurred a debt of about $44,000.00

An appreciative William Patterson, the College's first president, told the State Superintendent of Education, "I desire to thank the citizens of both races for the moral and substantial aid given to the College during the past year; so, to the Governor and yourself, I offer my profoundest gratitude."

Even during these difficult days, while the Civil War was a bright and bitter memory and the promises of Reconstruction had not been met, the black citizens of Montgomery stepped forth to work for their own betterment. They set a precedent that would be followed by their offspring, in the middle of the next century.

In 1955, Alabama State College's financial condition was somewhat improved, but it was still a segregated stepchild insofar as the Alabama State Board of Education was concerned. The state's per capita appropriation for black students was only a fraction of what was provided for the students at the all- white University of Alabama at Tuscaloosa.

The fourth president, H. Councill Trenholm, who had succeeded his father, had won the confidence and praise of the state officials by his frugal management of the college's finances during the depression. At times, Trenholm had been forced to use the earnings of the College Band, the Alabama State Collegians, to make ends meet. At other times, he used script instead of money, when the state's inadequate appropriations ran out between paydays. Such ingenuity won Trenholm praise from educators as well as legislators. It was a reputation worth protecting.

A tall, bespectacled man, with a regal bearing, Trenholm was a participating, rather than a delegating administrator. He rarely gave anyone an assignment and left that person to his or her own devices. He remained "in touch" with his staff. Since he lived on campus, his habit of dropping in was, at times, disconcerting. As a result, he ran a tight ship and knew most of what was going on around the campus.

Robinson and her team were aware of the risks they were taking to invade the private property of a state school, seize control of its duplicating equipment and appropriate its paper to launch an unauthorized campaign against the state's segregation laws. Whatever misgivings they had, did not appear to impede their efforts.

Dr. Mary Fair Burks, in a conference paper, "Trailblazers: Women in the Montgomery Bus Boycott"[6] presented at Georgia State University in 1990, reflects on those fateful days back in 1955. She writes of Mrs. Parks' arrest, the printing of the leaflets, and especially of the role of the Women's Political Council.

The WPC was organized by Burks, in 1946, when the all-white League of Women Voters refused membership to black women. The WPC was a "woman power" organization formed to cope with any injustice, no matter what, against black people. In 1953, alone, WPC members were confronted with some thirty racial complaints against the city's bus company, brought by people in the community. Dr. Burks goes on to describe some of her own traumatic experiences, personal scars, and, to exacerbate it all, a trumped-up traffic violation.

"I was in my car," she writes, "just behind a bus, when the traffic light turned green. As I started to move the car, I saw a white woman attempting to get to the curb. After the woman stopped cursing me, I was the one arrested for using profanity."

"When the woman was pressured into making charges, I tried to explain that it was she and not I using the profanity. But I was stopped by a policeman's billy-club. Before being thrown into a cell, I insisted on my right to a telephone call. (Having just returned from my doctoral studies at the University of Michigan, I had learned such legalities.)"

"My husband came to the jail, accompanied by a family friend and a white lawyer who read the charge, tore it up, and demanded my release. There were no black lawyers at the time; but, if there had been, only a white lawyer could have torn up that charge and secured my release. Otherwise, I might still be in jail."

When Dr. Burks contacted the women whom she felt would and should be involved in a group working for change, she was pleased with the response. Almost everyone present at the first meeting had a similar, unhappy experience to relate to the group. Some of the WPC organizers, there from the beginning (unaware that they were making history as trailblazers of the Civil Rights Movement), included: Irene West, Zoeline Pierce, Thelma Glass, Albertine Campbell, Jewel Clayton Lewis, Ive Pettus, Mary Cross, Elizabeth Arrington, Cleonia Taylor, Faustine Dunn, Cynthia Alexander, L. Streety, Thelma Morris, Bertha Williams, Geraldine Nesbitt, Portia Trenholm, Sadie Brooks, Frizette Lee, and Ruth Vine. A later list included Uretta Adair, and in 1950, Jo Ann Robinson became a member. (Later, Adair and Robinson joined the board of the MIA.)

The WPC members all worked to become registered voters, not an easy task at the time, with all the efforts, legal and illegal, to deny blacks the vote. The group went on to establish city-wide, voter registration schools. They developed a plan for a Negro Youth City, working with Alabama State College's Laboratory High School and the Booker T. Washington High School. They also worked toward opening public parks to Negroes and, of course, they struggled with the problems of bus segregation.

Six months before the Rosa Parks' arrest, members of the WPC wrote a letter to the city's Mayor, W.A. Gayle, with three specific requests:

1. That buses stop at every corner of Negro residential areas, as they do in white communities.

2. That changes should be made in the allotment of reserved seats.

3. That the Montgomery City Lines bus company discontinue the practice of having Negroes pay at the front and go to the rear to enter.

Members of the WPC met with the Mayor and the City Commissioners on several occasions, to no avail.

When Dr. Burks resigned as president of WPC, she urged Mrs. Robinson to assume the position. Dr. Burks praised Robinson's work as president. She lamented that Robinson's involved and important participation in the Bus Boycott was for so long ignored. Dr. Burks, after reviewing Robinson's account of the boycott in her book, *The Montgomery Bus Boycott and the Women Who Started It,* advised others to read it.

Jo Ann Robinson had many times, discussed with friends and acquaintances some of her disdainful experiences, in particular the bus incident in 1949. It occurred just prior to her first Christmas in Montgomery. She had driven to Dannelly Field, Montgomery's airport, left her luggage for her trip planned for later that day. She then returned her car to her garage, so it would be secure, while she visited family in Cleveland, Ohio. After that, she boarded the Montgomery City Lines bus, headed for the house of friends who were also to travel.

Mrs. Robinson explained that there were only two other people on the bus and she, absentmindedly, took a seat near the front of the bus. Suddenly, she was aroused from her thoughts about the family and the trip by the driver, who was angrily ordering her to get up. He was standing over her, repeatedly shouting the words, with his hand drawn back as though to strike her. Shaken and frightened, she fled the bus in tears.

Ashamed and hurt by this 1949 experience, the memory remained fresh on her mind that early morning in 1955, as she struggled with the boycott leaflets. So this, in a way, was the culmination of some six years of vengeful planning by Robinson. This is why she sought entry into the College's business department and literally called "the boycott."

By the evening of December 2nd, many of the city's blacks had received the leaflets with word of the planned, one-day boycott. As the ministers got word from their members who saw the leaflets, they were bolstered in their own efforts. More than 50 people met in the basement of Dexter Avenue Baptist church. They represented every segment of the black community: ministers, doctors, lawyers, businessmen, teachers (primarily from Alabama State College), unskilled and semi-skilled laborers, students, heads of political, professional and social clubs, men and women, all were represented. Dexter Avenue Baptist Church was, and is, centrally located for such a meeting.

Earlier in the day, Nixon had asked Mrs. Parks to attend. After getting off from work she went to the church and was surprised to see so many enthusiastic supporters. She was requested to "tell the people what had happened on the bus." Rev. Hubbard presided.

After Reverend Hubbard opened the meeting with a prayer, Reverend Bennett arose, commented on the heroic stand taken by Mrs. Parks and restated the purpose of the meeting. He put forth the proposal that everyone must stay off the buses Monday, as an act of protest and urged everyone present to cooperate and spread the word to others.

Bennett took such a commanding role that he hardly gave anyone a chance to comment, ask questions, or offer any ideas regarding the mobilization of forces for the proposed boycott.

In a room full of leaders, men and women accomplished and adept in their own right, many of them believed they had worthwhile contributions or suggestions to make. The high-handed, autocratic manner in which Bennett conducted the meeting threatened to undermine the organizing effort before it could get started.

Some of the members left and others were on the verge of leaving. Only after "blistering protests" from some of those who remained, followed by Rev. Abernathy's takeover of the meeting, was the meeting salvaged and the group able to organize.

Even when order was restored, the group was not in agreement on all the issues discussed on the agenda. But one thing seemed certain, "Not once did anyone question the validity or desirability of the boycott itself." Everyone seemed to agree that some massive demonstration should take place to protest Mrs. Parks' mistreatment.[7]

With this crisis of collective participation resolved, it was decided that the following things should be done:

1. Notify everyone in the black community of the events that took place on the Cleveland Avenue bus on December 1, 1955.

2. Seek the cooperation of everyone to support the Bus Boycott of December 5, 1955.

3. Inform the public of Mrs. Parks' trial on the morning of December 5, 1955.

4. Make the Bus Boycott the only sermon delivered by the ministers on Sunday, December 4, 1955.

The business, civic, and professional leaders all formulated plans on how best to reach their respective patrons, constituencies, and associates.

Youth leaders eagerly consented to organize students and young people; they volunteered to carry the word urging people to stay off the buses. Secretly among themselves, some even vowed to act as enforcers, to keep people off the buses, if necessary.

Mrs. Parks recalled that, "Young people preferred to act rather than to discuss and have speeches and listen to speeches."[8]

It was decided to draw up another circular that was briefer and slightly different from the earlier one. Its message, however, was essentially the same:

> Don't ride the bus to work, to town, to school or anyplace Monday, December 5th.
>
> Another Negro woman has been arrested and put in jail because she refused to give up her bus seat.
>
> Don't ride the buses to work, to town, to school, or anywhere on Monday. If you work, take a cab, or share a ride, or walk.
>
> Come to a mass meeting, Monday at 7:00 p.m., at the Holt Street Baptist Church for further instruction.

A group of volunteers, including Robinson and her team, continued to mimeograph the new circulars during the church meeting. They were packaged in bundles for delivery to well chosen spots for city-wide distribution.

Early in the meeting, the method of transporting workers to their sites of employment was discussed. Special attention was given to those who had to travel great distances, and to the sick and infirm, who needed medical care. A suggestion was made to use black-owned taxi companies, if they would charge no more than the ten cent bus fare. Multiple fares would be encouraged for each taxi, improving the taxi company's possibility to make a profit. The more optimistic observers thought that the companies might earn more than usual with the multiple fares.

Reverend William J. Powell, pastor of Old Ship AME Zion Church, Montgomery's oldest black church, volunteered to take charge of the taxi situation. Reverend Powell was born in Crenshaw County and his family moved to Birmingham where he attended primary and secondary schools. He assumed the pastorate at Old Ship in 1954, a year before the Bus Boycott began and the same year that King came and Attorney Gray returned to Montgomery.

The recruitment and coordination of vehicular transportation became a vital factor in keeping high the morale of the thousands of boycotters. Rev. Powell was an excellent choice for that job.

In the weeks ahead, it was his strength of character coupled with skillful business-like administrative talents that proved to be a central element, "a vital disk in the backbone of the movement."[9]

The group decided to hold another meeting Monday night, after the boycott, to reassess the day's events. Reverend A.W. Wilson, a successful, middle-aged minister, had already offered his Holt Street Church as the place to hold a mass meeting. A small man, physically, he had a tough constitution and commanded great loyalty from his church members.

Reverend Wilson often displayed much sagacity in matters of political survival. On issues involving church or civic struggles, he was always in the right camp. For a long time, he had fought for racial justice and had been one of the leaders of the Negro Civic League, since the nineteen forties. Reverend Wilson had one of the larger congregations on the west side, and his Holt Street Baptist church was one of the largest and most modern edifices in town. The meeting would be open to everyone.

The Friday night meeting adjourned, successfully, with everyone excited about the tasks to be performed and the impending challenge to the city's racism.[10]

The next day, thousands of their new flyers urging people to stay off the buses Monday, were circulated. Irene West, Uretta Adair, Mary Fair Burks and other WPC members helped with the delivery. Frank Massey and a battalion of other students, acting as couriers, stuffed flyers into mail boxes and under doors. They rang doorbells, and stopped people on the street to tell them to stay off the buses on Monday. Ministers informed other ministers who were absent from the previous night's meeting, of the plan to boycott the buses. The news was disseminated from small shops, stores, restaurants, and social clubs owned by blacks. Staying off the buses Monday was the talk in the beauty shops, barbershops, pool halls, taverns, and at corner hang-outs.

Reverend Powell successfully contacted all of the taxi companies and most of the cab drivers. They agreed to meet with him at Jeremiah Howard's Funeral Home. Howard, proprietor of the mortuary, owned one of the larger cab fleets in the city, the Good Service Taxi Company. He was helpful in organizing the cab operators and providing the gathering place.

Reverend Joshua Hayes assisted Reverend Powell at the meeting; they were able to get the cooperation of all of the cab companies. The cab drivers would charge only ten cents per person from the hours 4 a.m. to 9 a.m. and from 3 p.m. until 11 p.m. Powell assured them that in all probability they would be carrying full loads on Monday.

Interestingly enough, the drivers and owners seemed willing to help in Monday's boycott and to transport passengers, not so much because they thought they might profit from it. To the contrary, they were concerned about the contribution they could make toward solving the bus problem. "All the black folks of this town were familiar with the injustice we had been subjected to," recalled Reverend Powell.

By late Saturday afternoon, the evening editor of the *Alabama Journal* carried the story that blacks were urging a boycott of the city buses on Monday. The newspaper noted that unsigned fliers "are being passed from door to door in the Negro section of the city" and commented upon the arrest of Rosa Parks Thursday night. Apparently J.H. Bagley, manager of the bus company, learned of the leaflets when a woman informed him that her maid had brought one of the flyers to work with her. Bagley went to the woman's home, secured the leaflet, turned it over to his company's attorney and made an announcement to the press. In essence, Bagley explained that his bus company was not exempt from obeying, city and state laws. "He was sorry that black people blamed his company for these laws which everyone had to abide by."[11]

Before leaving for his job, on Friday, Nixon had called his friend, Joe Azbell, of the *Montgomery Advertiser*, to inform him of the pending plan, a strategic move on Nixon's part, to get the word out.

It would be the first Sunday of the month, the one day when practically every church was assured of a full turnout. With all the church choirs present, the deacons on hand, and the church club leaders and their membership in attendance, it would be a propitious day to make an announcement. From every pulpit in every black church in the city, the call was to be, "stay off the buses Monday."

The front page of the morning's newspaper carried another story on the plan by blacks to boycott the city's buses. Joe Azbell, the column's author, reported that a "top secret" meeting was going to be held by the city's blacks at Holt Street Baptist Church, Monday night. There, they would receive "further instructions" regarding an "Economic Reprisal" directed against "segregation on city buses...." Azbell related the campaign to one "modeled along the lines of the White Citizens Council program," which was used against blacks who sought enforcement of the 1954 decision regarding school desegregation.

The writer reported that the message printed on the mimeographed fliers "flooded" the black community. Apparently the first circular distributed, the one produced at Alabama State College, was the one that was printed verbatim by the newspaper.

Joe Azbell reported that information on the boycott reached the newspaper Friday afternoon, when white women reported that their maids had asked for Monday off, so they could boycott the city buses, because "we have been asked to do it." Attempts made on Friday by the newspaper to discover what black leaders were behind the proposed boycott proved unsuccessful and were met with only the responses of "no comment" and "no knowledge."

Additionally, the newspaper disclosed an attempt to get Reverend A.W. Wilson to tell who was behind this protest, and who arranged for the Monday night meeting at his church. In spite of the pressure on him, Reverend Wilson refused to identify any persons, saying, "Under no circumstances will I give you the names." He clarified a misconception the newspaper held about the meeting, stating that it would be open to the public "and the doors will not be closed to Negroes or whites."

There was little doubt in anyone's mind that the reason the local newspapers printed these stories of the scheduled boycott was to expose to the white community what the black folks were planning. If any message was intended for the black community, it was to scare the black leadership and intimidate them from doing such a thing and to stop the people from following such "dangerous advice."

This white response through the news media, however, had a positive affect for the black community. It proved to be the first major mistake by those whites who wanted to stop the boycott. It helped to promote the boycott. Although the campaign to mobilize blacks to stay off the buses had been waged by many people through various ways since Friday, it was estimated that by Sunday, less than half of Montgomery's black citizens had been reached through these methods. But when the newspapers printed the story in their columns, they inadvertently promoted the Monday bus boycott like no other method could, reaching thousands yet unnotified.[12]

To publicize the details on the front page of the newspapers that blacks were going to boycott the buses, did more to help the cause than anyone expected, especially the whites who opposed the protest. It was a tactical blunder of immense importance.

Through this news report, many Negroes got word of the Monday plan for the first time, "The whole thing turned out to the Negro's advantage, since it served to bring the information to hundreds who had not previously heard of the plan." E.D. Nixon believed that the newspaper stories did "more to help bring the people together in Montgomery, with reference to the Bus Boycott, than anything else." In retrospect, some years later, he would chuckle, "We couldn't have paid for the publicity the white folks gave us free of charge."

By Sunday morning, December 4, 1955, word of the impending boycott had spread into the black community as a rumor of indefinite origin and authenticity. The few thousands who had attended the meetings or seen the boycott flyers were only a small fraction of those who must be enlisted for a boycott to even approach a successful execution. Church members, many consumed with bitter memories of racial harassment on the city's buses, flocked to the churches in droves, exceeding the usual first Sunday in the month increase.

The city's black ministers added news of the boycott to their morning worship service, in varying degrees. In some instances, an announcement was made and attention was called to the articles in the *Alabama Journal* and the *Montgomery Advertiser.* Ministers, especially those who had been a part of the earlier discussions, used the coming protest as the basis of their morning messages. They exhorted their flocks to "stay off the buses tomorrow." This command was reinforced by such Negro Spirituals as:

"Walk Together Children"

> Walk together children, don't get weary
> Walk together children, don't cha get weary
> Dere's gonna be a great camp meetin'

In de promised lan'

Walk and never tire
Walk and never tire
Dere'a gonna be a great camp
In de promised lan'

and "Joshua Fit De Battle of Jericho"

Joshua fit de battle of Jericho
Jericho, Jericho
Joshua fit de battle of Jericho
and de walls come tumblin' down.

Up to de walls of Jericho,
He marched with spear in hand;
"Go blow dem ram horns," Joshua cried,
"Kase de battle am in my hand."

Den de lamb ram sheep horns begin to blow
Trumpets begin to sound
Joshua commanded de chillun to shout
and de walls come tumblin' down

Dat Morning,
Joshua fit de battle of Jericho
Jericho, Jericho,
Joshua fit de battle of Jericho
and de walls come tumblin down.

"Tomorrow morning," many ministers charged their departing parishioners, "We'll fit de battle of the buses and the walls of racial segregation will come tumbling down."

FOUR

Monday, December 5, 1955

Monday morning arrived and the black people of Montgomery, Alabama stayed off the buses en masse. Martin Luther King, Jr., who thought the boycott would be a success if only 60 percent of the people rode the buses, was surprised and overjoyed when he observed that the buses ran empty. He could see from his living room window that one of the heaviest routes frequented by black passengers, the South Jackson Street line, had no black riders. Wanting to investigate the matter further, he jumped into his car and drove around the city. He could not believe his eyes. "I was jubilant," King wrote. It soon became "apparent" to him that the Bus Boycott was "almost 100 per cent" effective.[1]

No other words could explain it. "A miracle had taken place. The once dormant and quiescent Negro community was now fully awake." Similarly, an AME Zion minister who arose early to observe the boycott, would later record:

This first phase of the beginning of a new age for an oppressed people in the Heart of Dixie bore an outward sign of victory although a long, hard struggle lay ahead. There was almost complete consensus that this was the time the Negroes should take a firm stand for their freedom. We have proven to ourselves that we can stick together. We have shown the white people that we can stick together. Let us stand firmly until they know we mean business. Such statements were on the lips of the Colored citizens milling about the streets. Many of these people took a holiday, their only reason being, "We want to celebrate."[2]

61

The city made another costly mistake by placing all of the police in Montgomery on alert for duty. Practically every police vehicle in the department was in use. Police were assigned to trail the buses to insure that black people were not restrained from riding the buses by those promoting the boycott. Other policemen were ordered to patrol the "main bus stops." Police Commissioner Clyde Sellers declared, "I intend to make certain that law and order are maintained today, even if we have to call out every city policeman and every reserve policeman." The commissioner said that he would post "policemen at every bus stop and anybody who wants to ride the buses can do so with the police department's assurance they will be protected." A boycott by black people of the buses was seen as a "most serious matter," and the police department was determined to handle it as such. The motorcycle policemen, in particular, "buzzed up and down the streets and remained near most buses as they entered Negro sections."

Some of the boycotters made the rueful observation that when they really needed police protection against vicious bus drivers who were deputized to enforce segregation, the police were unresponsive to their cries for help.

Interestingly, some prospective black passengers, persons who had either not heard of the boycott or desired to take the buses anyway, when they saw the empty buses approach, trailed by police cars, mistook this as a sign of intimidation coming from the white authorities not to take the buses (to keep away from the vehicles); and they made no move to board them. Seeing other policemen standing at the bus stops, many blacks refused to go to those waiting stations. They continued walking or took an alternate means of transportation to work.

Consequently, those black persons who may have ridden the buses that day were inadvertently prohibited from doing so by the ominous presence of the police. The city's effort backfired.

How ironic, the police, the primary instrumentality used to maintain and enforce the status quo, as did the newspapers, became a promoter of the Bus Boycott.

One black person, Fred Daniels, was arrested by two policemen at 7 A.M. on the corner of Holt and Thurman Streets for allegedly stopping a black woman who was about to board a bus. He was charged with disorderly conduct. Another account maintains that Daniels, a college student, was just helping an elderly woman cross the street when he was arrested by the police.[3] No other example of alleged threats of violence to prevent people from catching the buses was discovered that day.

Unquestionably, over ninety percent of the black riders had cooperated with the planners. The police reported that by 7 A.M., only two blacks had gotten off buses and approximately four or five had boarded at the Court Square stop, the major bus depot downtown. Usually, the buses were packed with Negroes going and coming at that time. A bus driver reported that "The one black person who rode his bus trembled with fear." The few black riders tended to be the elderly.

In a rare scene, a black woman stood alone, waiting for a bus, while other blacks stared at her. She said that she thought the whole thing was "silly." As if needing to explain or rationalize to those around her what appeared to them to be a treacherous act, she exclaimed: "I've got to work if I want to keep my job and my young ones come before all of this mess.... If anybody fools with me, I'll crown 'em," raising her umbrella, threateningly.

To be sure, such acts of defiance were few and far between, that morning. In the main, throughout the day the buses carried only white passengers.

It was a magnificent sight. A flood of black folks, young and old, men and women, filled the streets and sidewalks enroute to their designations. A reporter witnessing the scene, observed, "None spoke to white people." In fact, little talk was exchanged among the blacks themselves. It was an event almost solemn.

Many people got rides with friends or strangers. Some drove their cars and picked up others along the way. A few people with cars, having no place in particular to go, volunteered their services, becoming instant, on-the-spot chauffeurs. Others metamorphosed into jitneys. Blacks were on almost every corner waiting for rides. Some stood patiently, others paced back and forth to keep warm in the windy, frigid weather.

People getting in and out of cabs at intersections, became a common occurrence. Some cabs, packed with riders in the front as well as the rear seats, followed the bus routes. They dropped off passengers and picked up new ones at various stops, as if they were the city's authorized transportation service.[4]

Black school children walked to school, many of them accompanied by their parents. With haughty disdain, they turned their backs to the buses when the vehicles approached.

An unexpected and, indeed, unusual sight was the number of white women who employed black cooks, nurses, maids and other domestic servants, who drove into the black community to fetch their black employees. More than likely, this response was due to the story appearing in the newspaper which stated that blacks who worked for white people as maids and servants had informed their employers on Saturday that they would not show up for work on Monday unless the employer came for them in an automobile or agreed to pay their taxi fare.

It was also reported that at least one, "white man was carrying Negroes in his automobile and parked in the downtown area until he got a load." Off-duty black GI's from the nearby military bases, pitched in and helped, transporting people to their destination.[5]

The vehicles used by Negroes that day remained a sight to behold, a parade of humanity never to be forgotten. People got rides in old pickup trucks; some took bicycles and carts to work. Many a poignant scene became ingrained in the memory of passers-by. It seemed as if here was a reenactment of "The General Strike." One observer recorded, "Men were seen riding mules to work, and more than one horse-drawn buggy drove the streets of Montgomery that day." Some had short distances to travel. Others would walk up to twelve miles in the crisp cold weather. The sight of this mass movement, of silently marching blacks, influenced others not yet persuaded, to join the protest.

People stopped to watch the big, empty, yellow buses of the Montgomery City Lines pass them by. They resisted the temptation offered by some, now friendly drivers, to get on board. One witness recorded that, "as the day progressed the boycotters began to cheer the empty buses, laugh and make jokes."

Martin Luther King, Jr., in eloquent terms, summed up what appeared to many to be a phenomenal event in the history of these people, "They knew why they walked, and the knowledge was evident in the way they carried themselves. And as I watched them, I knew that there is nothing more majestic than the determined courage of individuals willing to suffer and sacrifice for their freedom and dignity." The long march had begun in Montgomery, Alabama.[6]

By 9 o'clock that morning, as Mrs. Parks approached the courthouse where her trial was to be held, she could hardly enter the building. At least 500 people filled the sidewalks, streets and entrances trying to get in to see the proceedings.

They cheered Mrs. Parks on. Many offered their services and stood ready to help her if the need arose. "The steps leading into the north side of the courtroom and the sidewalk, along with the corridors leading into the east entrance of the courtroom, all were jammed with spectators and witnesses."[7] Reporters were admitted to the courtroom, but before and during the trial photographers were not permitted to take pictures.

At the Recorder's Court hearing, the prosecutor, Eugene Loe, moved to alter the charge against Mrs. Parks, making the warrant read that she violated state law instead of the city ordinance. Attorney Gray objected to this action, but Judge John B. Scott allowed the charge. Gray then countered with the argument that this state law was not a city law, therefore, it did not apply to Mrs. Parks. Loe replied that the state law applied to all transportation. The city had eleven witnesses on hand to testify in its behalf, but only three were called to the stand.

The bus driver, J.F. Blake, was called to the stand and he briefly told the Court that Mrs. Parks refused to move from her seat when ordered to do so. Two women also testified. One of them said that there was a seat in the back of the bus that Mrs. Parks could have taken but that she refused to take it. This statement apparently contradicted the testimony given by the bus driver who said that "there were twenty-two Negroes and fourteen whites seated in the 36 seat bus," making doubtful the availability of another empty seat for Mrs. Parks to move to.

This former testimony was produced by the city attorneys to prove that Mrs. Parks had violated the current rule by remaining in what had now become the white section of the bus. They stated that a vacant seat was available for her in the reduced black section. The court chose to ignore the testimony of the bus driver who had stated that there were no other vacant seats behind where Mrs. Parks was sitting.

Rosa Parks' stubborn defiance challenged two other conventions:

1. No black person could remain seated, anywhere on the bus, if a white passenger was standing, and

2. All of the seats in a row had to be abandoned by black passengers even if only one white passenger elected to sit on that row.

Mean-spirited, white youth often took advantage of this ruling by taking seats in the black section, forcing blacks to move further to the rear, even if no seats were available. With her brazen, public demonstration of defiance against the status quo, its guardians could not allow Mrs. Parks to win her case.

Attorney Gray lost the case. Mrs. Parks was found guilty of violating a state law requiring racial segregation on city buses. She was fined $10 plus a $4 court cost, $14 in all. Gray, with Nixon's concurrence, proceeded to file an appeal. Both he and Nixon signed the $100 bond for Mrs. Parks' release.

As they left the court, well wishers continued to give moral support to Mrs. Parks and encouragement to Fred Gray and E.D. Nixon to fight on. "When we turned to go through that door," remembered Nixon, "we couldn't hardly walk. Black men were crowded in that place all the way back to the street around there."

Nixon emerged from the courthouse, alone. Mrs. Parks and Fred Gray were left behind, temporarily, to sign papers and clear up a few additional matters. Fearing for Mrs. Parks' safety, the crowd yelled, "If you don't bring her out in a few minutes, we're coming in after her." Nixon could hardly believe his ears; for such challenges had never been heard before. "It was the first time I had seen so much courage among our people!" recalled the Pullman porter.

Police stood outside the courthouse, "armed with sawed-off shotguns." It seemed to Nixon that they were "just wanting some of us to do something, so they would have an excuse to shoot down black people. Other police stood guard on the rooftops and stared out of the windows of nearby buildings, ready for action."

Nixon tried to calm the crowd, saying, "Everything is all right, keep calm, because we don't want to do anything to make that man use the shotgun." The master organizer cautioned the crowd not to hang around, "because all they want is some excuse to kill somebody." The well-disciplined crowd melted away.

Another confrontation, potentially more violent, had been averted. E.D. Nixon could not help but remember that on many other previous occasions he had been the only person on hand at the court house to stand by and defend the rights of black persons, who unjustly came before the law. "But the morning we tried Mrs. Parks," he recalled, "the black man in Montgomery came into his own and stood on his feet as a man."[8]

When the crowd disbanded, E.D. Nixon, Ralph D. Abernathy, and Edgar N. French met to discuss the morning's developments at the office of the Home Missions, Brotherhood, Pensions and Relief of the AME Zion Church. Over the weekend, the leaders who had met at Dexter Avenue Baptist Church, Friday night, had decided (primarily at Abernathy's insistence), to hold a private meeting among themselves at 3:00 o'clock before convening the larger, public gathering scheduled for later that evening.

Nixon asked what was to be discussed at the earlier meeting. Abernathy informed him that they were going to meet to discuss the Bus Boycott. Both Nixon and French concurred that they would need to do "more than... talk" about the boycott. Nixon believed that they should formulate a policy for the future course of action and present it to those meeting in the afternoon.

Apparently Nixon had already composed a list of demands he thought should be made on the bus company and put to the group for consideration. Aside from these, he recommended the formation of a new organization to represent the interest of the community, and he had "a man in mind" to lead it. The ideas of Nixon and French constituted the core of the proposals to be put forward. French drew up the following memorandum:

We, the Negro citizens of Montgomery, shall continue to register our protest against man's inhumanity to man, and no one of us shall ride any city bus until the Montgomery City Lines company agrees to:

1. Allow all patrons, white and Negro, to be seated on buses on a "first- come, first-served" basis. Negroes will be seated from the rear toward the front. White people will be seated from the front toward the rear. There are to be no signs or lines of

demarcation and no one is to be asked to give up a seat.

2. Give assurance that Negroes will be accorded all the courtesy afforded any other patrons of the city lines and that no abusive and insulting language will be used by the bus operators. Negroes are to be guaranteed a dime's worth of service for a dime.

3. Since a large percentage of the bus patronage is Negro, Negroes who qualify should be employed to operate buses running into predominantly Negro sections.[9]

All three men agreed on the resolutions. They felt that the boycott should continue until these demands were met, and they agreed to work together to persuade the others to adopt the plan.

At the three o'clock meeting held at Reverend L. Roy Bennett's Mount Zion church, many more people were in attendance than had been present at the Friday night meeting. Everyone was overjoyed that the one-day boycott had been a success.

Questions soon arose. Should they remain off the buses on Tuesday? What should they tell the people who would be at the Holt Street Baptist Church that night? And many other inquiries came to the floor. Word had reached Abernathy, the convener of this meeting, that some "Uncle Toms or other persons would take the message of their meeting back to the white community." Rumor had it that "some spies had come in." In order that their plans not be leaked to the white authorities, Abernathy proposed that an "Executive Committee of 18 persons" be empowered to go to the pastor's study and do the work the larger gathering was originally supposed to do and report back to the larger body once a plan of action had been formulated.[10]

Off in the pastor's study, in the large room that served, also, as the National Headquarters of the AME Zion pension fund, Nixon presented the body with the proposals he, Abernathy, and French had drawn up earlier. For two reasons, Abernathy suggested that the leaders form a new organization. He recalled that because Reverend Bennett (the logical man to spearhead the drive since he headed the Interdenominational Ministerial Alliance) had nearly blown the Friday night meeting, a new organization and leader were necessary. If the movement was going to have a successful beginning, he thought it would be wiser "to take it out of Reverend Bennett's hands, because he was going to flunk it!" explained Abernathy. Apparently, many others shared this view.

Rufus Lewis, a coach at Alabama State College and a successful businessman, agreed that Reverend Bennett's handling of the previous meeting had "confused many people." Prince E. Conley believed that this man (Bennett) "did more harm to the movement than good." Conley felt that they needed, "to think of somebody who could, do a more effective job in presiding over the meeting."[11]

Second, the other logical entity through which people could be mobilized, the local NAACP chapter, was a weak organization; it was really not attracting anybody, particularly the masses of people. Consequently, the group came to accept Abernathy's proposal that a new organization would be needed, other than the NAACP.

One conclusion of the earlier meeting was that this was to be an ad hoc organization with aims limited only to the immediate bus problem. Abernathy, however, proposed that it would be a "permanent organization that would deal with this problem and similar problems in the future." Some leaders "felt that a new organization was really necessary to give life and meaning and vitality." So it was agreed to make it a new and permanent organization.

Due in part to the composition of those attending this meeting, the new organization was made up of the presidents of the federated clubs, representatives of labor unions, the leaders of the various social and civic associations, and the ministers.

In fact, the ministers made up the largest single block of those in attendance, and they "dominated" the meeting. Yet, all of these persons were involved in the decision-making, and all would make important contributions to the movement.

Nixon suggested that the new organization be called the "Montgomery Citizens Council," but Abernathy felt that the name sounded too much like the White Citizens Council, an extremely segregationist organization with which they eschewed even the slightest association or comparison. Abernathy's suggestion of the Montgomery Improvement Association (MIA) was readily accepted.

Rufus Lewis immediately nominated Dr. King to be president and made a nice speech for him. Prince E. Conley quickly seconded the nomination. No one put forward another name, and there was no debate. The motion was put to a vote, and Martin Luther King, Jr, was unanimously elected president of the Montgomery Improvement Association. The motion "carried because nobody had anything against Dr. King," recalled Abernathy, "we were just trying to get a leader."[12]

Dr. King, in recounting the sequence of events, wrote that it happened so quickly that he "did not even have time to think it through." Had he had a chance to think about accepting this new office, it is, "probable that I would have declined the nomination." Only a few weeks earlier, he had refused to be considered a candidate to head the local NAACP. He wanted to devote more time to his church. Work on his dissertation, which he had only recently completed, had taken him away from the full assumption of his pastoral duties. Then, too, his wife, Coretta, had just had a baby girl, Yolanda, and the thought of spending more time with his family, no doubt, entered his mind. Moreover, King was a "Rufus Lewis fan." He knew that Lewis was well-trained and would be a "good spokesman for the black community."[13]

Abernathy was also taken unawares by the election of his

close associate, Reverend King. Although King and Abernathy had become great friends since King's arrival in Montgomery, he had not thought of King to head the MIA. They had been together Friday night, on Saturday, and at Mrs. Parks' trial earlier that morning where they had talked about a possible substitute for Reverend Bennett. But it was far from each of their minds to consider each other, or themselves, as a suitable replacement for Bennett.

Therefore, Abernathy was "surprised, pleasantly so" by the choice of Dr. King, but he felt badly that he "had not been the one to offer his name. I had not even said to him, why don't you take the presidency," Abernathy admitted later.[14] Since King had discussed the matter with him, Abernathy was well aware of King's plans to concentrate more time and energy to his church work.

Neither did Abernathy consider himself for the presidency of the new organization. For different reasons, he too, like King, had turned down the offer to head the NAACP. He was planning to go away to school for further study and was reluctant to assume any additional responsibilities. Furthermore, Abernathy was a "Nixon fan." He believed that, "Mr. Nixon was fearless and bold and would really stand up to the white power structure." He considered Nixon to be the best man to lead the black community at this hour of crisis. Although King, "was a Lewis fan," and Abernathy, "was a Nixon fan," neither of the two ministers was strongly opposed to either person.[15]

Because of its significance for the remainder of this story, the election of Martin Luther King, Jr., to head the Montgomery Improvement Association, requires further consideration.

King was new in the city and unknown by most black Montgomerians. Even at this December 5th meeting, only a few of those present were closely acquainted with him. Although committed to improving the conditions of black people, he was not the most socially or politically active black minister in town. Neither was he identified with any faction and he had not made any enemies.

A biographer has suggested that King was not, "the most radical" person, but that he, "made a handsome appearance...."[16] One historian has written that King was, "sufficiently naive, or brave, to accept designation as the exclusive leader of the boycott." However, a careful examination of this meeting yields other insights; and perhaps, a brief consideration of the views of others closer to the scene may add an important dimension to the election.

To begin with, Rufus Lewis said "that he nominated King because he wanted a man who could do an effective job in getting the organization going. King seemed to talk with more sense." Lewis, a member of King's Dexter Avenue Baptist Church, had high regards for his pastor. He had heard Dr. King speak and was moved by what appeared to be the young minister's leadership capabilities. Furthermore, Lewis recognized that King was "young enough to put enough energy into this thing and succeed."

Yet, at the same time, Lewis was forced to admit that, "Nobody knew at the time what sort of man he was." Perhaps, more important than Lewis' laudatory assessment of King was his opposition to other possible candidates. He knew that there were "two or three folks who wanted to be president, even the man who kept us confused wanted to be president," referring to Reverend Bennett. "We certainly did not want the man presiding at the time, to be president."

He also believed that "Nixon wanted to be president of this body." So, wanting to control the situation, Lewis had conferred with Conley, striking an agreement that when the propitious moment came, Lewis would nominate King and Conley would second his nomination.[17]

Nixon, in a later disclosure, claimed that he had planned from the outset, that King should head the movement. Nearly three months earlier, Nixon heard King speak at a NAACP meeting held at the Metropolitan church. "King didn't talk about 'pie in the sky'," remembered Nixon, "he was talking about what people do in the community." Nixon was so inspired by the oratory and carriage of the young minister that he told James E. Pierce, there and then, "I don't know how I'm going to do it, but some day I'm going to hang him to the stars."

Now, during the weekend of December 3, 1955, Nixon came to the conclusion that King would be a good person to head the boycott. So when Abernathy asked him, at the meeting with Reverend French, if he was going to be president of the new organization they were considering, Nixon told them that he would consider the position only if everyone rejected his choice for the office. Nixon knew King to be "a very intelligent man." However, Lewis nominated King before Nixon had the chance.

Attorney Fred Gray, opined that "Martin Luther King, Jr., was not the leader of the movement. He was merely selected to head the organization which spearheaded the movement. There were several leaders who contributed to and gave direction to the protest. King should better be viewed as the spokesman for those dozen or so persons." Elaborating on this view, Gray said that "no one doubted his ability, but Dr. King was selected to lead the movement as a compromise, essentially, between two opposing factions that were present at the meeting."[18]

On one hand, there was E.D. Nixon who had been a pioneer in the field for many years, who was considered the leader of the masses but not necessarily the classes. Then, there was Coach Lewis, who was considered the leader of classes and not the masses. Many people believed that if the movement was going to be successful, everybody was needed. To pick anyone of these two powerful and influential competitors to lead the organization might alienate the one not selected and keep him and his supporters out of the movement - a possibility having disastrous consequences which had to be avoided.

Moreover, Gray said that some in the group felt that, "if they had chosen either one of those two spokesmen, the Montgomery Improvement Association would have gotten bogged down with personalities." Therefore, they decided to choose King. Here was a "nice young man," new in the community, who had not become identified with any political group.

Another prominent member of the organization offered a different interpretation of why King became the spokesman. Reverend B.J. Simms maintains that, "King was selected by the black leaders to be a scapegoat if the boycott failed." Many were fearful of what the white backlash to the boycott would be.[19]

Some were doubtful, indeed skeptical, about the probable success of a prolonged boycott, if it continued beyond this first day. They feared that the white power structure could crush them at will, and if the boycott was broken they would let King be the fall guy. King, they reasoned, was young and had a long future. They did not want to jeopardize what little time they had left, on a venture that might fail. He was not rooted in the community, and had no deep investments here as had others. "We've got to live here; he can leave if necessary," was sometimes heard. If necessary, they reasoned, King could always return to Atlanta and pastor at the successful church of his father, Martin Luther King, Sr. He had a place to go; they did not, if the authorities cracked down on them.

These comments are but a sample of the uncertainties that clouded the group's organizational efforts. The most remarkable fact is that under the circumstances they were able to reach this early consensus on their choice for a leader.

Regardless of the different motives behind the selection of Martin Luther King, Jr. to head the Montgomery Improvement Association, one thing was certain, "Nobody had anything against Dr. King... we were just trying to get a leader. And we did not think that it would go much further than Montgomery, you know, at the particular time," commented Abernathy.

Other officers were elected at this meeting: Reverend L. Roy Bennett became the first vice president; E.D. Nixon was chosen treasurer; Mrs. Erna A. Dungee accepted the position of financial secretary; Reverend Uriah J. Fields became the recording secretary; Reverend E.N. French became the corresponding secretary; Reverend Ralph D. Abernathy accepted the position as director of programs; Reverend William J. Powell headed the transportation committee; and Fred D. Gray was in charge of the legal affairs. All the others present would constitute the Executive Board.

Having spent so much time in the preliminaries, not much time was left to prepare a proper agenda for the larger meeting that was soon to follow. At first there was a difference of opinion as to the type of meeting to have. Some suggested a typical prayer meeting where unsigned, mimeographed instruction would be passed out to the audience.

While it was clear that the black community had sent an unmistakable message that it was ready to challenge the power structure of the city, some of the leaders were not sure they wanted to be identified personally, with this oncoming assault. Already, they knew that the press would attend the meeting from distant cities as well as Montgomery. Their fear of informers who reported everything to the white community was a constant threat to any activity that was considered radical. For a moment or two, the future of the group hung in the balance.

E.D. Nixon, increasingly angered by what he described as "cowardice" among some of the ministers, jumped to his feet and demanded silence, using language that was not ordinarily heard in church. He exclaimed, "How in hell are you going to have a protest without letting the white folks know about it!" In a chiding voice, Nixon asked, "What's the matter with you people? Here you've been living off the sweat of these washwomen all these years, and you haven't done a thing for them. And now, you've got a chance to pay them back. But you're too damn scared to stand up on your feet and be counted. The time has come when you men is going to have to learn to be grown men or scared boys. I think you're acting like a bunch of cowards!"

Nixon's blistering rebuke brought forth a chorus of disclaimers of cowardice and a willingness to prove it. They met Nixon's challenge for direct action. Nixon remembered that King was one of the first to speak, "Nobody can call me a coward! Come on, let's roll up our sleeves and get down to work!"

From that moment onward, King, assisted by many, moved to the forefront of the Montgomery Improvement Association to provide courageous, creative leadership to the Bus Boycott. Nixon's timely challenge had given renewed courage to those who were seeking a short cut to freedom.[20]

The group, no longer hobbled by doubt and indecision, got down to work to prepare and present a plan of action to their highly charged constituents. Expectedly, despite Nixon's encouragement and King's acceptance of leadership, some shadows of doubt lingered that required serious attention.

The three demands drawn up at the earlier meeting with Nixon, French, and Abernathy were presented to and approved by the group. Additional suggestions were made to have bus drivers call black police to the scene of bus disputes when they occurred in black neighborhoods, and to "run every other bus special for Negroes, on the predominantly Negro routes." But these supplemental demands were later dropped.

Some still thought their point had been made with the one-day boycott. They argued that it was better to call a halt to the protest while it was successful, rather than let it die out in a day or two as enthusiasm waned and be ridiculed by its failure. However, the majority felt that the boycott should continue until the city met the demands.

Fred Gray prepared a contingency plan in the form of two

resolutions. One resolution simply stated that if they did not get the type of support they were hoping to get from the people, they would call off the protest. The other resolution stated that even if they got the support but felt that they could not hold out over an extended period of time, they would tell the people and the bus company officials that the protest was only meant to last for the day. This successful day of protest would then be cited as an example of, "what was to come," if their demands were not met and conditions on the buses did not improve.[21]

Both factions concurred that confirmation of a future plan of action could not be had until the mood and disposition of the people were assessed. No firm decision to continue the boycott could be made until these ideas were presented to and approved by the masses of Montgomery's black citizens, soon to convene. The committee adjourned with the future of the boycott hung in the balance.

With this meeting adjourned, no one was quite sure of the future course of the Bus Boycott. Their moment of truth was at hand. The first day's defiant response had clearly demonstrated the residual power that the black community could muster through unified action. Never in the history of the town had blacks been shown so much courtesy and respect by the policemen and such salutation by white bus drivers.

One of the oft-told tales that reflects the altered mood of the time was that of a bus driver who stopped to allow his only passenger, a black man, to exit in a black neighborhood. Through his rear-view mirror, the driver saw an elderly black woman, supported by her cane, hobbling hurriedly in his direction. He smilingly, leaned out the door and said:

Driver: "You don't have to rush, auntie. I'll wait for you."

Woman: "In the first place, I ain't your auntie. In the second place, I ain't rushing to get on your bus. I'm jus' trying to catch up with that nigger who just got off, so I can hit him with this here stick." She gestured menacingly with her walking stick.

The unprecedented show of unity and force, by the black community was so unusual that the leaders did not know the strength of their own commitment and feared overplaying their hand.

On the other hand, all of them had been victimized, one way or another, by the racist power brokers that they were preparing to confront. Unlike the group who had fought successfully for an end to school segregation the year before, this group had no national leaders or strong organizations on its side. The team being put together to speak for the community had never worked together before and was being chaired by an outsider who was relatively unknown. Yet, a charged public was already gathering for action. These are some of the thoughts that apparently troubled the group as they prepared for the mass meeting.

King raced home from the afternoon meeting to Coretta and Yolanda, sometime after 6 o'clock. He informed his wife that he had been drafted as president of the new protest committee. Much to his relief, she did not object. King had no time for supper; he had to leave for the mass meeting within one half hour. He went into his study and closed the door, wondering how he could possibly create such an important speech in a few minutes when he required fifteen hours to prepare an ordinary sermon. He had written only a few notes on a piece of paper, when it was time to go.[22]

Martin Luther King saw the gathering hordes, heard the buzz of their excitement and felt the mood of their impatience and hope as they flowed into the church and its environs by the thousands. He, as much as anyone there, realized that this movement had already passed the point of no return. The only thing needed was direction. Fate had placed that burden on his shoulders.

One must wonder, however, how King's assessment of the black community as a newcomer to Montgomery affected his mood and the content of his speech on this day. Earlier, King had found several things which he felt needed to be remedied in the city. In *Stride Toward Freedom*, he describes, "an appalling lack of unity among the leaders."

King acknowledged that several civic groups existed but felt that each was at loggerheads with the other. "Not only was the community faced with competing leadership," he stated, "but it was crippled by the indifference of the educated group. This indifference expressed itself in a lack of participation in any move toward better racial conditions and a sort of tacit acceptance of things as they were. To be sure," King added, "there were always some educated people who stood in the forefront of the struggle for racial justice, but they were exceptions. The vast majority was indifferent and complacent."

"Some lack of concern", he said, "was due to fear, but much was due to sheer apathy." He further added that "even in areas of voting, the educated group had an indifference that, for a period, appeared incurable."[23] Now, we see King catapulted into a position of leadership with the opportunity to do something about what he referred to as "an appalling lack of unity."

From what we have seen and what was to come, it would appear to this author that King initially misread the community. It is hard to imagine any other black community mobilizing as Montgomery's blacks did and carrying out the boycott in such a disciplined and dignified manner and with such determination.

FIVE

Monday Night

In the early afternoon of Monday, December 5th, even before the leaders convened their preparatory meeting at Mount Zion Church, many blacks began arriving at Holt Street Baptist Church. Some came to the meeting place directly from work. By 7 p.m. the church was packed. The overflow crowded near the entrance, on the lawns and porches of nearby homes and filled the streets within six blocks of the church in every direction. A massive traffic jam clogged Cleveland Avenue, a major artery where vehicles normally moved smoothly. As parking space diminished and traffic congestion increased on the streets approaching the church, motorists double parked, abandoning their cars to rush to join the throng heading for the church. Thousands of people were turned away or gave up hope of ever being a part of the proceedings as they encountered the tumultuous crowd.

Virginia and Clifford Durr, who started out early for the meeting had to turn back. Virginia Durr recalled that they "couldn't get within three or four blocks of the church. Thousands of people surrounded the church." Emphasizing the popular turn-out to this mass meeting, she said, "There was no way we could get close to the church much less to the mass meeting. I suppose there were 10,000 people around that church."[1]

Holt Street Baptist Church had loudspeakers attached to the outside of the building. Reverend Wilson had the public address system turned up so those standing outside (far more people than were inside the church) could hear the proceedings.

When the meeting began, the police ordered Reverend

81

Wilson to cut off the public address system charging that it was disturbing the peace. He refused to do it. They asked him again to turn it off. Reverend Wilson then took the police to the system's control center and told them, "if it gets cut off, you'll have to cut it off." The police, after surveying the crowd, backed down. They refused to touch the controls, perhaps fearing a massive attack on their outnumbered forces if they tried to prevent those in the street from hearing what was taking place inside the church.[2]

With Reverend Bennett presiding, the mass meeting began with the hymns, "Onward, Christian Soldiers" and "Leaning on the Everlasting Arms." To one observer, "when that mammoth audience stood to sing, the voices outside swelling the chorus in the church, there was a mighty ring like the glad echo of heaven itself."[3]

Reverend W.F. Alford, pastor of Beulah Baptist Church, led the congregation in prayer. Reverend Uriah J. Fields followed with a passage from the Bible. Then E.D. Nixon took the podium and began his remarks with a prophetic warning, "My friends, before all of you get comfortable in your seats, if you're afraid, you'd better get your coat and hat and go home now."

"This is going to be a long, drawn-out affair, and before it's over, somebody is going to die! It may be me! It may be you! But if I die, the only thing I ask is don't let me die in vain. But it's going to be a long, drawn-out affair."

Nixon's sobering words reminded them of the seriousness of their actions, something of which they must always be cognizant. His comments brought everyone to the edge of his seat as he urged them to be steadfast and determined to win respect and justice on the buses.

Before leaving the rostrum, somewhat indulgently, he engaged the group in honest self-criticism. Nixon chided them saying, "You've been getting up every morning putting on an apron so that you'll have a lap to beg in. Today we're going to throw this apron aside and stand on our feet and take our rightful places in society like men." As Nixon departed from the podium, "the people screamed."[4]

Then Martin Luther King, Jr., took the pulpit to give the main address. First, he told what happened to Mrs. Parks, four days before. Next, he retraced, episode after episode, the injurious, oppressive and shameful treatment others had suffered on the buses. After a pause, he warned "But there comes a time... when people get tired. We are here this evening to say to those who have mistreated us so long that we are tired, tired of being segregated and humiliated, tired of being kicked about by the brutal feet of oppression."[5]

His words seemed to arouse the passions of the people like no other. The church went wild with applause at this statement. But King went on, saying, "We had no alternative but to protest... For many years, we have shown amazing patience. We have sometimes given our white brothers the feeling that we liked the way we were being treated. But we come here tonight to be saved from patience that makes us patient with anything less than freedom and justice."

A chorus of "Amen" and "Well" accompanied these remarks only to be drowned out by the enthusiastic applause which followed. King justified the protest on moral and legal grounds, commenting that, "One of the great glories of democracy is the right to protest for right." To dispel any association between their methods and those of the Ku Klux Klan or the White Citizens Council, he maintained that "these organizations are protesting for the perpetuation of injustice in the community. Their methods lead to violence and lawlessness. But in our protest there will be no cross burnings. No white person will be taken from his home by a hooded Negro mob and brutally murdered. There will be no threats and intimidation. We will be guided by the highest principles of law and order."

Although King had not previously enunciated his philosophy of nonviolence, it had been a vital factor in his training for the ministry. In this, his first public speech before an organization that he would lead for the next 13 years, this reach for nonviolence was evident.

In no uncertain terms King said, "I want it to be known that we're going to work with grim and firm determination to gain justice on the buses in this city." Moreover, to reassure the people, in carefully measured phrases, King affirmed: "And we are not wrong; we are not wrong in what we are doing. If we are wrong, the Supreme Court of this nation is wrong. If we are wrong, the Constitution of the United States is wrong. If we are wrong, God Almighty is wrong. If we are wrong, Jesus of Nazareth was merely a Utopian dreamer and never came down to earth. If we are wrong, justice is a lie."

The church shook with deafening applause. Those inside and outside the church went wild with enthusiasm upon hearing these words. King and the congregation established an immediate community of aspiration and expectation for action. He told them what they were waiting to hear. Equally important, they knew that he spoke from conviction and with the fearless, unselfish commitment of a true leader. He was ready to lead, and they were ready to follow.

On the heels of this call to "militant action," Martin Luther King, Jr., counseled the people not to force anyone to stay off the buses and interjected into his speech a few words of caution. In part, these words contained the germinating philosophy that in time would underlie the ideology of the movement. He maintained that the method of this movement would be "persuasion, not coercion." The only constraint or inducement permitted would be to "let your conscience be your guide."

Martin Luther King, Jr., told the congregation what he firmly believed, that "our actions must be guided by the deepest principles of our Christian faith. Love must be our regulating ideal." Reciting the words of Jesus Christ, he advocated, "Love your enemies, bless them that curse you, and pray for them that despitefully use you." In giving this advice, the young preacher earnestly thought that, "If we fail to do this our protest will end up as a meaningless drama on the stage of history, and its memory will be shrouded with the ugly garments of shame."

Therefore, his counsel urged that: "In spite of the mistreatment that we have confronted, we must not become bitter, and end up by hating our white brothers."

In concluding his speech, King passionately reaffirmed to all those who came out that night that, "we are determined here in Montgomery to work and fight until justice runs down like water, and righteousness like a mighty stream. And we prepare ourselves for what lies ahead. Let us go out with a grim and bold determination that we are going to stick together." Again and again cries of "Amen" and "Hallelujah" were shouted to the rafters. Cries of agreement and praise crashed and intermeshed with foot-stomping and deafening applause from the floor.

With determination never before countenanced among Negroes in Montgomery, King spoke these words: "We are going to work together. Right here in Montgomery, when the history books are written in the future, somebody will have to say, 'There lived a race of black people, of people who had the moral courage to stand up for their rights. And thereby they injected a new meaning into the veins of history and civilization.' And we're going to do that. God grant that we will do it before it's too late."

Pandemonium broke out. The place went up for grabs. The church women rocked with emotion and screamed from their seats. Some deacons nodded and others waved their arms in approval. People jumped to their feet with excitement and cheer. Thunderous hand-clapping and foot-stomping shook the church to its foundation. On the outside and in the streets, a tumultuous cry and applause rang out, disrupting the quiet, cold, wintry night air as if a tremendous explosion suddenly went off, warming, electrifying and illuminating the darkness. This was, without a doubt, as King himself would later put it, "the most decisive moment of my life."

If there were any who doubted his ability to lead, their fears were soon dispelled after this speech. To Eugene Ligon, "This was the awakening... It was the most stimulating thing I have ever heard. Nobody dreamed that Martin Luther King being that sort of man under these conditions."[6]

If there were any (and we can be safe in assuming that there were many ordinary folk in this category) in the congregation who questioned why this newcomer (and not one of the older, established, proven ministers) was making the main address, their inquiries were soon put to rest by this deeply moving address. As Rufus Lewis put it, "This was the time that the people were brought face to face with the type of man that Martin Luther was, not only the people who came to the mass meeting, but those who selected him, too. That was the great awakening. It was astonishing, the man spoke with so much force."[7] In time, the people would come to ask not "who is Martin Luther King, Jr.," but "why not Martin Luther King, Jr.?"

Reverend King was surprised that his words were so well received, and, with typical humility, he was "thankful to God" for it. Furthermore, the young preacher noticed that his address had accomplished the difficult task of "combining the militant and the moderate" voices of protest, by no means an insignificant achievement. As he would record, there could be no mistaking the fact that, "The people had been as enthusiastic when I urged them to love, as they were when I urged them to protest." To be sure, "The question of calling off the protest was now academic," wrote King. "The enthusiasm of these thousands of people swept everything along like an onrushing tidal wave."[8]

Next, the resolution, drawn up earlier, was read to the assemblage by Ralph Abernathy. The essence of the statement called for blacks to stay off the buses until three basic demands reiterated to the bus company were met. The first item demanded that courtesy be extended to all black riders by the white drivers. The second item demanded that the seating policy be changed to a first-come, first-serve basis, with blacks beginning in the rear and whites beginning in the front; and wherever they met, this would be the dividing line. There would be no seats reserved for white passengers. Black passengers would not have to stand up over empty seats, and the drivers could no longer demand that blacks yield their seats to white passengers and move to the back of the bus. The third demand required the bus company to employ black bus drivers on the predominantly black routes.[9]

The resolution was overwhelmingly approved, without dissent or question.

Recalling the moment, E.N. French wrote: "An insatiable thirst for freedom had seized everyone. A new dignity and a new destiny had been conceived,"[10] It was, indeed, an amazing development for "nobody expected such a response," wrote L.D. Reddick.[11]

Before the meeting ended, a collection was taken. Money was given freely and generously to help further the cause and, as one observer noted, "without the usual money-raising salesmanship."

Fred Daniels, who had been arrested that morning for having stopped a woman from boarding a bus, was introduced to the congregation, and everyone gave him a hearty, uproarious applause.

Rosa Parks was presented and was given a resounding ovation, lasting several minutes. It was her resolute act of resistance that moved people to stay off the buses that historic day. It was her brave defiance, of segregation, that brought the people to Holt Street Church that memorable evening. As King observed, "she was their heroine. They saw in her courageous person the symbol of their hopes and aspirations."[12]

Black resentment against Rosa's arrest was not only due to this one incident, but it was the "straw that broke the camel's back."

For E.D. Nixon, Rosa Parks was "the catalyst." For Reverend S. Seay, she was the only one to "spark the opportunity for... staying off the bus which had been talked about for so long before." Reverend E.N. French could not deny that, "A strange sense of community and group consciousness seized each person present. Not only was Mrs. Rosa Parks arrested, but every Negro in Montgomery felt arrested." Reverend French succinctly summed up what appears to have been the prevailing mood, "In every heart and mind was the thought that now we must register our protest against the inhuman, unchristian, unlawful and unethical indignities which we have suffered through the years."[13]

Likewise, to L.D. Reddick it seemed that, "Almost everybody could tell of some unfortunate, personal experience that he, himself, had seen." One conclusion that could be reached from this show of respect to Mrs. Parks and this phenomenal response was that "Montgomery Negroes were fed up with discriminatory bus service in particular and, like Negroes throughout the South, with bad race relations, in general... Negroes, themselves, wanted to get into action. Here and elsewhere, they were willing to fight it out..."

What, then, is one to make of these events, beginning with Rosa Parks' determined stand Thursday evening and culminating in the mass meeting four days later? For one thing, although there would be many variations over the next twelve months, the basic theme of this protest was soundly established by the conclusion of this mass meeting at Holt Street Baptist Church. The leadership, for the most part, had coalesced; an organization had been formed, and the people supplied the driving force.

L.D. Reddick interpreted the movement as being a "massive" reaction of the black community. With the careful skill of a disciplined social scientist, he wrote:

Martin Luther King did not precipitate the Montgomery bus strike; that was done by Mrs. Rosa Parks. Neither did he think up the idea of the boycott. Credit for that must go to an unidentified professional man and a teacher. King did not create the Montgomery Improvement Association but was himself chosen by the MIA. Nor did he impose his will upon the organization; rather, most of its decisions were the results of collective thinking.

Above all, the impulse and stamina of the boycott movement came from the thousands of Montgomery Negroes - the cooks and maids, the laborers, skilled and semiskilled workers, housewives and students - who were regular bus riders. They were the people who picked up and swept along their leaders and bore them up whenever the morale of the leadership sagged.[14]

The explanation given by E.D. Nixon was simple yet basic to understanding what had happened. "It was something, really something," he said. "And they come out of the low income bracket, they were working people. Hardly any could be seen from the professional fields that day." The Pullman porter, at a loss for words could only state that, "This thing had been blown up and blown up until everybody got fed up with it. This was a popular 'black revolt', kicked off by the catalytic act of Rosa Parks."

Clifford Durr saw it as a popular mass movement, the likes of which he had never seen before. "The leaders were saying, we stayed off the buses all day. Wasn't that wonderful? We showed 'em!" he recalled. "But the reaction of the cooks and the maids was, 'We ain't showed them nothing yet. We ain't going back on those buses until they start treating us right.' It was the masses of blacks that shoved the leaders into the boycott, extending it."

Reddick labeled as absurd the notion, heralded by some newspaper reporters at that time, that the NAACP, particularly the central headquarters in New York City, had anything to do with starting the boycott. In fact, it should be noted that the NAACP was not fully in agreement with the process or goal of the boycotters. W.C. Patton, the NAACP representative in Alabama, was sent to Montgomery to study the situation. He met with Fred Gray, Mrs. Parks, and then with King and asked them about reports that the group was seeking only a better form of segregation. King told him that they were trying to solve an immediate crisis with the first-come, first-serve seating plan. Gray made it clear that this was only a tentative arrangement.

But, in New York, Roy Wilkins, NAACP National President, instructed Mr. Patton that the NAACP could not, "at present, assist in any appeal of Mrs.Parks' conviction on account of the MIA's seating proposal. The NAACP could not join in on any other basis than the abolition of segregated seating on the city's buses." Wilkins continued, "They are just asking for more polite segregation." Later, when the scope of the boycott included complete integration of the buses, the NAACP became an active participant in the struggle.[15]

Regardless of what later would be written about these early developments, the judgement of another participant deeply involved in the boycott, seems rather convincing. Reverend B.J. Simms has commented that:

> The lower economic blacks were the ones who really demanded a better way of life. And those of us who were better educated and civic minded joined in to help them. Because no matter what their numbers might mean, the poor, the depressed, the uneducated can never successfully lead a revolt. You must have leadership.

There had been other blacks such as Reverend Seay and Nixon fighting the battle together with some of our more prominent women in their women's clubs trying to do something about it. But until Rosa Parks... resisted that Thursday afternoon it sparked something among the principally... lower economic group of blacks. And then those of us who had some better training, by the grace of God, stepped in to help them. I've often wondered if we had not, we might have had a blood bath here in Montgomery.[16]

There was no doubt that some saw this as a revolt in the making. Ralph Abernathy wrote that "Mrs. Parks ignited a spark which began the modern-day revolution. She did this when she would no longer cooperate with the system of segregation on the city buses and refused to obey a white bus driver to give up her fourth seat so that one white man could sit down, on that first day in December." And, not surprisingly to Martin Luther King, Jr., who would often refer to this seminal event throughout the remainder of his life, nothing would be clearer:

"We moved black people into the southern streets to demand that their citizenship and manhood be respected. Considering that we were in the South, with such a complex system of brutal segregation, indeed, we were inaugurating a rebellion. For merely to march in public streets was to rock the status quo to its roots."

And, so on they walked, day in and day out, through winter, spring, summer, and fall.

Lerone Bennett, *In What Manner of Man,* addresses the question asked by so many, as they look back on what happened in Montgomery. What made it work? He concluded that what made Rosa Parks' act significant and the Montgomery Bus Boycott so compelling was the ambience of the age.

"Negroes were ready for a new shuffle of the cards. Events, the interior migration of the 30s, and the 40s, and the convulsion of the 50s, had prepared them. Basic to an understanding of

Montgomery and of King," he says, "is an understanding of this fact: Negroes had already changed. They only needed an act to give them power over their fears, an instrument to hold in their hands and a man to point the way."

"Montgomery furnished all three," says Bennett, "giving Negroes not only an act but, also, a remarkable fisher of men and a new ideology, nonviolence. King must be seen as a leader who solved a technical problem that had worried Negro leaders for decades. As a powerless group, dominated by a powerful majority, Negroes could not stage an open revolt. To go into the streets, under these conditions with open demands for change, was suicidal. King solved the technical problem by clothing a national resistance movement in the disarmingly appealing garb of love, forgiveness, and passive resistance."[17]

At that time, King was a man who had heard of and read about Mahatma Gandhi, but who was not yet a full-fledged Gandhian. While at Crozer Seminary, a few years previously, King talked of guns and self-defense, and of battle, but he would also say that Negroes would never win their freedom by using violence. In his classes, King had mostly studied religious philosophers and the words of Jesus; but one day, he was unexpectedly introduced to Gandhi, when he heard a lecture on the Indian leader by Dr. Mordecai Johnson, president of Howard University. This was a most important and enlightening speech, and it caused a profound and life-long change in King's entire outlook.

In his speech on Monday night, December 5, although King did not mention Gandhi by name, he did explain his theory of civil disobedience to the people in terms they could understand. "These explanations were crucial; because one can't expect people to undergo pain and humiliation without having very good reasons to justify suffering."[18]

Abernathy felt that King supplied those reasons with clarity and authority. Although it was not until later in the boycott that King got a deeper understanding of the demands of Gandhism, it was this consideration and introduction that was crucial to the success of that moment. Since earlier boycotts had degenerated into violence, it was crucial that this one was launched from a platform of nonviolence.

To Abernathy, because of their mutual insistence that the protests be peaceful and nonviolent, he and King made a good team. "If we were to win," he said, "we would have to gain the sympathy of the nation by exemplifying the Christian principles we profess, even if it meant being reviled, beaten, and possibly killed."

Lerone Bennett writes of the critical letter to the editor of the *Montgomery Advertiser,* from white librarian, Juliette Morgan, outlining the similarity between the Montgomery struggle and Gandhi's crusade. King was impressed by this comparison, which was fully in accord with his thinking at that time.

Morgan, a victim of the rejection and condemnation of the white community after her letter was published, died in the summer of 1957. Before she died, the name of Gandhi was well known in Montgomery. People who had never heard of the little brown saint of India were now saying his name with an air of familiarity.

Nonviolent resistance had emerged as the technique of the movement, while love stood as the regulating ideal. In other words, King explained, "Christ furnished the spirit and motivation while Gandhi furnished the method."[19]

King, as he embraced the concept, turned the Negroes' church-rooted faith toward social and political understanding by melding the image of Gandhi and the image of the Negro preacher. Then he combined it with Negro songs and symbols.[20] Embracing the ideas of William Lloyd Garrison, King learned that the history of mankind is crowded with evidence proving that physical coercion is not adapted to moral regeneration; the sinful disposition of man can be subdued only by love; that evil can be exterminated from the earth only by goodness; that there is a great security in being gentle, harmless, long-suffering and abundant in mercy; that it is only the meek who shall inherit the earth, for the violent who resort to the sword are destined to perish with the sword.[21]

As the boycott unfolded, the inspiration of Gandhi began to exert increasing influence on King. He had come to see early that the Christian doctrine of love, operating through the Gandhian method of nonviolence was one of the most potent weapons available to the Negro in his struggle for freedom.

King, as he became a more serious Gandhian scholar, stated that his skepticism concerning the power of love gradually diminished. He came to see for the first time, its potency in the area of social reform. Prior to reading Gandhi, he explained, he had concluded the ethic of Jesus was only effective in individual relationships. The "turn the other cheek" philosophy and the "love your enemy" philosophy were only valid, he thought, when individuals were in conflict with other individuals. When groups and nations were in conflict, he thought, a more realistic approach seemed necessary. After reading Gandhi, King realized that he had been totally mistaken.

It is interesting that few were ever totally committed to Gandhi's philosophy; but, through nonviolence he challenged the might of the British Empire and won freedom for his people. Eventually, this provided the model for the success of King and all of Montgomery's black citizens.

The philosophy of nonviolence as described by King has five characteristics:

First, it must be emphasized that nonviolent resistance is not a method for cowards; it does resist. If one uses this method because he is afraid or merely because he lacks instruments for violence, he is not truly nonviolent. While the nonviolent resister is passive in the sense that he is not physically aggressive towards his opponent, his mind and emotions are always active.

A second fact that characterizes nonviolence is that it does not seek to defeat or humiliate the opponent, but to win his friendship and understanding. The nonviolent resister must realize that boycotts are not ends in themselves; they are merely means to awaken a sense of moral shame in the opponent.

A third characteristic of this method is that the attack is directed against forces of evil rather than against persons who happen to be doing evil. It is evil that the nonviolent resister seeks to defeat, not the persons victimized by the evil.

In other words, the tension in Montgomery is not between white people and Negroes; it is between justice and injustice, between the forces of light and the forces of darkness. And, if there is a victory, it will be a victory not merely for 50,000 Negroes but a victory for justice and the forces of light. We are out to defeat injustice and not white persons who may be unjust.

A fourth point that characterizes nonviolent resistance is a willingness to accept suffering without retaliation, to accept blows from the opponent without striking back. Suffering, the nonviolent resister realizes, has tremendous educational and transforming possibilities.

A fifth point concerning nonviolent resistance is that it avoids not only external physical violence but also violence of spirit. The nonviolent resister not only refuses to shoot his opponent, but also refuses to hate him. At the center of nonviolence stands the principle of love.[22]

Reverend Glenn E. Smiley, a white official of the Fellowship Reconciliation of New York, and a devout believer in Gandhian nonviolence, said of King, "I believe that God called Martin Luther King to lead a great movement. But why does God lay such a heavy burden on one so young, so inexperienced, so good? King can be a Negro Gandhi or he can be made into an unfortunate demagogue destined to swing from a lynch mob's tree."[23]

SIX

Barriers & Successes

During January and February of 1956, whites in Montgomery stepped up their efforts to destroy the effects of the boycott movement. Montgomery's Mayor Gayle joined the White Citizens Council as did numerous whites. There were 6,000 members on February 1, and by the end of February there were close to 12,000 members. The entire County Board of Revenue, as well as the three city commissioners, became active members of the Council.

Some of the white businessmen, worried about the residual effects of the bus boycott, formed a group, Men of Montgomery. They opposed prosecuting the black leaders and made several attempts to talk the leaders of the Montgomery Improvement Association into ending the boycott.

On February 13, Circuit Solicitor William Wretford, disagreeing with the tactics of the Men of Montgomery, pushed for a meeting of the grand jury to consider indictments against the boycott leaders. On February 21, the grand jury indicted eighty-nine blacks, including King and twenty-four other ministers, for conspiring to boycott. This action received national attention, something the Men of Montgomery wanted to avoid.

King was put on trial first. Atlanta attorney, A.T. Walden, called Thurgood Marshall, then general counsel for the NAACP, and Arthur Shores, NAACP counsel in Alabama, both of whom assured King that he would have the best legal protection.

The trial was set for March 19. Friends from all over the country, including Charles C. Diggs, Jr., Negro Congressman from Michigan, came to Montgomery to be with King. Wretford attempted to prove that King had disobeyed a law by organizing an illegal boycott. The defense attorneys: Shores, Peter Hall, Orzell Billingsley, Fred Gray, Charles Langford, and Robert Carter argued for the defense. Judge Eugene Carter, on March 22, declared King guilty of violating the state's anti-boycott law. The penalty was a fine of $500 and court costs.

Although this 1955 confrontation is looked upon as the time of the premier struggle against segregation in intrastate transportation, there was, in earlier times, a potpourri of major confrontations throughout the South. New Orleans, Louisiana, offers an early case study where Negroes were pioneers in protesting segregation in the city's streetcars and buses.

It was no accident that New Orleans was foremost among southern cities where black protest against segregation in public transportation began soon after the Civil War. Black political clout in Louisiana, especially in New Orleans, exceeded that in most other southern states and cities. Louisiana was readmitted to the Union on condition that the state would never amend its constitution to deprive its new (black) electorate of the franchise. This new constitution was written by a Reconstruction legislature whose lower House was one-half black. The constitution outlawed slavery and guaranteed "equal civil, political and public rights to all citizens without regard to race, color or previous condition and that public conveyances and places of business would be open to everyone."

During Reconstruction, Louisiana, unlike Alabama, had three black Lieutenant Governors, one of whom, P.B.S. Pinchback, served as Governor for a month. There was also a Secretary of State, a State Treasurer, a Superintendent of Public Education, and a United States Congressman, all black with political clout.

Although black protests began before the Civil War ended, a more serious attack was launched after black politicians were elected and the constitution was ratified. The story of their struggles, written by Professor Roger A. Fischer, set forth in the

Journal of Negro History, in 1968, is called, "The New Orleans Streetcar Controversy of 1867.[1]

The streetcars had been a source of irritation for New Orleans Negroes since they were first placed in service on the streets of the city in the 1820s. A few of the street railroad companies operated special cars for colored passengers. Other lines excluded them altogether. In rare instances, Negroes were permitted to ride on the regular cars, much to the disgust of many of the white passengers. The sight of two, "overdressed Negro wenches" riding on a Dryades Street vehicle in 1861 prompted an outraged white woman to ask of the New Orleans *Daily Crescent,* "If the omnibuses are for negroes, why not say so! If for white people, it is important that it should be known." But with few exceptions, the New Orleans streetcars remained strictly segregated throughout the ante-bellum period.

The Negroes resented this practice bitterly, for it caused them considerable inconvenience and afforded them a constant reminder of their inferior station in society. Uncommonly free from the deferential demeanor exhibited by most ante-bellum Negroes south of the Ohio, the New Orleans colored community made no secret of its discontent. In July 1833, several Negroes on their way to Lake Pontchartrain were refused passage on a car reserved for white traffic. They forced their way onto the car and a furious battle broke out between the Negroes and the white passengers, carmen, and bystanders. The colored intruders were finally driven from the car, but they soon returned with pistols and threatened the life of the driver. But the New Orleans Negroes lacked the power to change the rules and regulations of a society built upon slavery, and manifestations of their discontent were largely limited to such sporadic eruptions of violence.

Negro hopes were raised when New Orleans fell to the Union invaders in April 1862. A delegation of prominent free people of color called upon occupational commander Benjamin F. Butler and asked him to desegregate the city's streetcars. General Butler, the, "Beast" of local legendry, ordered the omnibus lines to accommodate colored passengers, but the directive was challenged by the car companies and set aside by a local court. Butler was removed in December 1862, and his successor, Major General Nathaniel P. Banks, allowed the ruling to stand. During the summer of 1864, in response to complaints from his own colored troops, Banks was able to persuade the street railroads to allow Negro soldiers to ride on the white cars, but colored civilians remained restricted in their car travel.

The cars operating on Baronne Street allowed whites and Negroes to ride on the same cars, but segregated the races by providing separate inner compartments. Although whites complained of indiscriminate mingling on the upper deck, this method apparently satisfied most travelers and removed the necessity of car duplication. But most of the omnibus lines operated totally separate cars for whites and Negroes. To eliminate possible confusion, they embellished the front, rear, and sides of each car designed for colored passengers with large stars. The cars operated for white travelers were left unmarked. Negro cars were almost always referred to as, "star cars," and the term, "star" soon became a local label for all varieties of segregated Negro facilities, much as the term "Jim Crow" would be adopted by a later generation throughout the country.

Negro leaders intensified their struggle against streetcar segregation in January 1865. The *New Orleans Tribune* founded by brothers Louis and J. B. Roundanez in 1864 as the first Negro daily newspaper in the United States, began to give the streetcar issue saturation coverage. Charles E. Logan and Dr. R.W. Rogers urged the formation of a committee to draft a memorial to military authorities to protest, "the restrictions imposed upon the colored people, preventing them from riding in the city cars." One Negro spokesman thought it, "a shame that a colored soldier be received in the cars, and his mother be expelled." Captain W.B. Barrett demanded "that no distinction be made between citizens and soldiers." The colored Union officer urged Negroes, "We must claim the right of riding for every one of us, and claim it unconditionally."

Negro demands met with temporary success in August 1865, when General E.R.S. Canby, Banks' superior since the disastrous Union defeat at Mansfield in 1864, issued an order that, "the attempt to enforce police laws or regulations that discriminate against the Negroes by reason of color, or their former condition of slavery... will not be permitted." The *Tribune* exultantly informed its readers that, "the distinction between 'star cars' and 'no star' is no longer of any value," and reported that colored passengers were being admitted, "with little or no difficulty" on all of the omnibus lines in the city. The hosannas proved premature, however, for once again the car companies took the matter to the courts. Only two weeks after the Canby order had been put into effect, it was invalidated by United States Provost Judge Benedict, who ruled that the edict infringed upon the basic right of a private corporation to refuse service to any group or individual it so desired. Once again one-third of the cars were decorated with stars and segregation prevailed.

The "star" system worked to the disadvantage of colored travelers, for while they were severely limited by their exclusion from two-thirds of the cars in the city, their own "star cars" were often taken over by impatient whites. Taking note of this situation in November 1864, the New Orleans *Daily Picayune* warned, "White persons can ride in the 'star' cars if they choose, but they have no right to object the presence of darkeys there." In September 1865, "A Citizen" reported to the New Orleans *Times* that on Sundays the cars operating on Canal Street - white and "star" - were often taken over completely by white travelers, thus excluding the Negroes. This condition was not alleviated, for the

New Orleans *Crescent,* certainly no advocate of equality between the races, pointed out in May 1867, that "It constantly occurs that white men, women and children fill the star cars, to the exclusion of colored persons, and it is a spectacle frequently seen, that white people occupy the seats in these cars, while colored persons of both sexes are compelled to ride standing in the aisles."

The streetcar segregation controversy was finally settled in the spring of 1867, after it had become the focal point for racial unrest that threatened to set off city-wide rioting between the races. In April, the *Tribune* intensified its militant campaign against the "star car" system. Chiding the segregationists for their backwardness, the *Tribune* declared, "All these discriminations that had slavery at the bottom have become nonsense. It behooves those who feel bold enough to shake off the old prejudice and to confront their prejudiced associates, to show their hands." Radical Republican orators and organizers, eager to channel black discontent into a massive bloc vote, found streetcar discrimination an excellent topic for inflaming the passions of their colored audiences.

On Sunday, April 28, words gave way to actions. William Nichols, a Negro, tried to force his way onto a white streetcar and was forcibly removed by starter Edward Cox. Nichols was arrested for a breach of the peace, but two days later City Recorder Gastinel, hoping to avert widespread trouble, dismissed the charges against the Negro on the grounds of insufficient evidence. But Nichols, who apparently incited the fracas to bring streetcar policies into the courts, was unwilling to let the matter rest. He promptly countersued Cox for assault and battery.

The Cox-Nichols incident triggered a chain reaction of Negro attempts to challenge the color line on the white streetcars. This presented the car companies with a delicate dilemma, for they wanted to retain segregation without running the risk of violence or lawsuits. Omnibus authorities tried to resolve the problem by a policy of "passive resistance." Streetcar personnel were ordered not to assault colored intruders, whatever the provocation, but they were instructed not to start the car on its destination until the Negro tired of the game and voluntarily departed. This strategy was put to a practical test on Friday, May 2, when Negro P. Ducloslange boarded a white streetcar on St. Charles Avenue. Ducloslange was not ejected, but the car remained stationary. Some of the white passengers departed when the Negro boarded, others left during the filibuster, and it then became a contest of endurance between Ducloslange and the driver. After a considerable delay, the Negro departed and the car proceeded on its route, empty but victorious.

The weekend of May 4-5 brought New Orleans to the brink of race warfare. On Saturday a bellicose crowd of colored men and boys gathered on Love Street, in the Third Municipal District, and began harassing the passing white cars by shouting curses, blocking the street, and showering the cars with a variety of projectiles. One of the leaders of the mob, a Negro named Joseph Guillaume, jumped aboard a white car and defiantly refused to leave. When the enraged driver forgot his instructions and tried to eject the Negro bodily, Guillaume overpowered him, seized the reins, and began to make off with the streetcar as a trophy of war while the terrified passengers evacuated as best they could. Guillaume was finally cornered by Third District police after a spirited chase and taken into custody.

The mob grew uglier, and the arrival of the police only seemed to make matters worse. Sergeant Strong of the Third District Station reported to Chief of Police Thomas E. Adams that, "squads of colored men, fifteen or twenty in a gang, armed with clubs, are gathering on Love Street, jumping on the cars and making threats toward the drivers." A short time later, Officer Kiernan, desk clerk at the Treme Station, described the disturbance to Adams as, "a large crowd of colored men in open riot." City police units from neighboring stations reinforced the beleaguered Third District lawmen, contained the mob, and prevented the violence from spreading. But tensions remained intense. A *Crescent* reporter thought the "public mind" to be "in a very feverish condition during the day, apprehensions having possessed people that a serious, perhaps calamitous disturbance might come upon the city, as a result of the continued agitation of this car question."

On Sunday, May 5, the unrest reached its climax. Early in the morning D.M. Reid, superintendent of P.G.T. Beauregard's New Orleans and Carrollton Railroad Company, relayed reports he had received from way-station personnel to Mayor Edward Heath that, "threats have been made by colored persons that they intended to force themselves on the cars reserved for white persons... and that should the driver resist or refuse them passage, they would compel him to leave the car and take forcible possession themselves." Convinced by events the day before that this threat would lend to, "much danger or riotous conduct," Reid urged the Mayor to take all possible precautions to, "insure the preservation of the public peace."

Despite the strong possibility of violence and destruction, Reid and other omnibus officials decided to keep their cars running and to maintain their strategy of passive resistance. That policy was put to the test early in the morning when two colored women boarded a white streetcar and adamantly refused to leave, causing the white passengers to disembark in disgust. The driver, faithfully executing company procedure, refused to continue on his route and the increasingly familiar battle of patiences began. But this confrontation went to the Negroes. After some delay, the driver succumbed to his impatience and drove the two triumphant women to their destination. A few more Negroes tried to ride in the white cars with less success, but by and large the morning passed with surprisingly tranquility.

That afternoon the smoldering resentments of generations of second-class status flamed into open violence throughout the city. A band of colored men tried to force their way on to a white streetcar on Canal Street, but they were driven off by an equally determined group of white passengers after a savage struggle. A gang of twenty Negroes jumped aboard a white rampart streetcar, overpowered the white travelers, and forced the terrified driver to parade them past wildly cheering throngs of their fellow protesters. A lone Negro vaulted onto another white omnibus, encouraged by choruses of "stay on, stay on" from the colored onlookers lining the sidewalks. Another gang of Negroes tried to take possession of a white car, but were turned back by a single white Union soldier, who reportedly told the Negroes that he had a mother and sister, and would not tolerate this insult to the white ladies on the car. Throughout the city, scattered fights broke out between roving bands of whites and Negroes.

As the news of the disturbances traveled, inevitable transformations took place in the throngs of people, white and black, who ventured forth onto the streets. The less bellicose white New Orleanians stayed away from the likely battlegrounds, particularly the streetcars. Angry gangs of white men and boys roamed about in search of colored cadres on which to vent their wrath. A number of them armed themselves and boarded cars, riding in wait for a Negro attack. The colored mobs grew correspondingly larger and bolder, their mood uglier. Their sorties against the white cars were now carried out by small armies, wielding such weapons as clubs, bottles, knives, and occasional pistols.

The most massive of the colored crowds gathered together on rampart Street near Congo Square, the traditional assembly ground for Sunday slave dances during the ante-bellum period. Earlier in the afternoon some twenty Negroes had taken possession of a white streetcar after a pitched battle and had coerced the driver to chauffeur them back and forth in front of a cheering crowd. The excitement brought other Negroes to the scene and still more were called from passing "star cars" to join their rapidly swelling ranks. Soon an estimated five hundred colored protesters were milling angrily in Congo Square, laying siege to every unfortunate white streetcar that came their way. A number of the Negroes boarded the cars, rode triumphantly for a few blocks, then returned to rejoin the Congo Square festivities. Impromptu orators rose up wherever they could attract an audience, shrieking a gospel of hate and violence that the mob was only too willing to listen to and act upon.

At this point Mayor Edward Heath decided that the time had come to intervene. Awakened that morning by a note from railroad executive D.M. Reid urging him to take all measures to, "insure the preservation of the public peace," Heath had kept a careful watch over the disturbances that now threatened to get out of control. Now a decision had to be made. He might have done nothing, hoping that the riot would burn itself out. But Negro emotions seemed to be intensifying, not diminishing, and the less reputable white elements might soon step in if the officials did nothing. He could have called in more policemen, but he realized that his local lawmen lacked the manpower to crush the disturbance and their presence might only further inflame the Negroes. His ultimate resort was the Federal forces garrisoned in New Orleans under his good friend General Philip Sheridan, commander of the Fifth Military District. The troops certainly had to power to quell the riot, but Heath, a moderate Republican, evidently feared the political repercussions from the powerful Radical faction in Washington, who were certain to be displeased at his use of Federal soldiers against the Negroes. Rejecting all of these alternatives, the Mayor courageously decided to go to Congo Square and reason with the mob personally. If words failed, then and only then would force be summoned.

Since his appointment to the mayoralty by Sheridan a few months earlier, Heath had won a well-earned reputation for fair play among the Negroes of New Orleans. It now served him well. He pleaded with the multitudes to disperse and return to their homes before a bloodbath similar to the disastrous disturbance of July 30, 1866, was touched off. He promised the Negroes that the proper authorities would re-examine streetcar policies immediately and that their case would be given full consideration. Heath's pledges were greeted by a few grumbles from the group, but its martial spirit had been broken. Soon Congo Square was empty. The peace had been preserved.

On the following day Mayor Heath, General Sheridan, and railroad representatives met to settle the matter. Car company spokesmen asked Sheridan to support the "star" system on their lines with Federal soldiers, but the hero of Cedar Creek flatly refused their request. The executives then withdrew and met by themselves to forge out a common racial policy. They stood to lose a considerable volume of white business if they mixed the races, but they ran the greater risk of losing their property and even more traffic if the Negro disorders were to continue. Finally they took the line of least resistance and abandoned the "star" system altogether. That evening, omnibus drivers and starters were instructed to permit travelers of all colors to ride the cars. To prevent further fracases on the cars between the races, Chief of Police Adams warned sternly, "No passenger has the right to eject any other passenger, no matter what his color. If he does so, he is liable to arrest for assault, or breach of the peace."

The actual death of streetcar segregation came more slowly. On May 8, the *Daily Crescent*, reported, "very little change" in Negro riding habits. According to the *Crescent*, "Nearly all of the colored travelers still go in the star cars, and even wait for them though a car for whites may be passing or present." Two days later the same newspaper informed its readers that colored passengers, "of their own volition, still take the star cars. The cases of Negroes entering the cars hitherto assigned to whites are exceptional." But gradually the exceptions became the rule, as the meeker Negroes followed their more adventurous cohorts onto the mixed cars as soon as they realized the havoc would not ensue. After a few weeks the stars formerly designating Negro cars were painted over.

The white New Orleanians accepted streetcar desegregation remarkably well. On May 10, a relieved company spokesman informed a *Crescent* reporter that the omnibus lines were experiencing, "little difference in the amount of travel on the city railroads since the distinction between cars has been abolished." On the night of May 20, a gang of white men armed with pistols and clubs forced their way aboard several mixed cars in the vicinity of the levee and ousted the colored passengers, injuring one rather seriously. Then the turmoil abated.

Explanations of the causes of the confrontation were varied. The Democratic press did not overlook the splendid opportunity to reap a political harvest, and accordingly laid the blame at the feet of the Republicans. As the *Daily Picayune* saw it, "the more impetuous of our colored population" had been prodded into actions so unbecoming their lowly station by, "the few Radicals in our midst, who would move heaven and earth, if possible, to revolutionize society for their own personal aggrandizement." Striking the same chord, the *Times* inveighed against, "vindictive and avaricious adventurers" who, "have poured the leprous distillment of dissatisfaction"into the ears of, "the ruder and more reckless portion of our Negro population."

These accusations were not without their germ of truth. Radical Republican organizers had descended in large numbers upon New Orleans in the spring of 1867 to capture Negro allegiance and they soon found the streetcar issue a ripe topic for their purposes. But these evangelists of the Stevens-Sumner gospel were more likely catalysts than creators, for the Negro resentments had been there a long time before there was a Republican party. The moderate *Crescent,* which placed the brunt of the blame on those inconsiderate whites who usurped Negro seats on the "star cars," may have come closer to the truth. But the fundamental cause was most probably the basic conflict between Negro status and Negro aspirations. The "star car" system had symbolized white supremacy itself, the traditional order of things in an age when many whites had been masters and most Negroes had been slaves. That era had been buried at Appomattox, and New Orleans Negroes saw the Union triumph as their chance to elevate themselves to full equality with all the prerogatives of first-class citizenship. As the *Tribune* explained during another struggle against segregation two years later, "under the present order of things, *our manhood is sacrificed.* The broad stamp of inferiority is put upon us. So far as the present custom goes, we are treated as pariahs of the country." Thus the colored crusade against the "star cars" was at bottom a broader and deeper quest for human dignity itself.

Contemporaries disagreed on the importance of the controversy they had just witnessed. The *Daily Crescent,* giving too much attention to the tumult and too little to the underlying issues, reported with relief that the matter had been put to rest, "and the probability of a collision of races averted." The *Times* noting that the "star cars" had been identical to the white ones, disgustedly dismissed the whole incident as, "a clamor for shadows." Even the *Tribune,* the Negro newspaper which had led the agitation against the "star" system, dismissed its downfall as "minor" and began to campaign against segregation in the public schools. But the militantly white supremacist *Daily Picayune* saw more clearly than its competitors that the car controversy was, "simply the introductory step to more radical innovations, which must materially alter our whole social fabric." Darkly hinting of a, "covert design in the whole movement," the *Picayune* ominously predicted that the, "sudden change... promises to assume a serious aspect as far as social tranquility and good order is concerned."

During the decade of Radical Reconstruction that followed, the *Picayune* prophecy was borne out, for the streetcar struggle proved to be precisely that, "introductory step to more radical innovations." Through the voter registration provisions of the First Reconstruction Act, the Radical Republicans came to power in Louisiana in the autumn of 1867, and New Orleans Negroes played powerful roles in the formulation of Republican policies. Some of them sat in the, "black and tan" constitutional convention of 1867-68, and prodded that assembly into prohibiting racial segregation in the public schools, places of public business, and common carriers. Other New Orleans Negroes guided through the legislature the enforcement bills that extended the constitutional bans on racial separation to the common law.

In rural Louisiana, where Radical authority was illusory and white shotgun sovereignty remained the law of the land, segregation survived without serious challenge. But in New Orleans the situation was altogether different. Under the protective aegis of a friendly Republican regime, city Negroes mounted determined campaigns against the color line in the public schools and places of public accommodation. They enjoyed little success in their drive to desegregate theatres, restaurants, and saloons, although a few of the more persistent pioneers did win the right to sit in empty galleries, eat salted food, and quaff drinks doctored with liberal doses of Cayenne pepper. A fairly substantial number of their sons and daughters attended the white public schools from 1870 to 1877. Segregation was eventually secured again by the Democratic restoration of 1877, but not before those, "radical innovations" prophesied by the *Picayune* had come to pass.

Negroes and whites continued to ride together in the same streetcars throughout the nineteenth century. While the white Orleanians defied school and saloon desegregation with every means at their disposal, they were strangely indifferent to the mixed omnibuses. Perhaps the New Orleans *Republican* was correct when it observed that it demanded, "a great strain of the imagination to make a mule car appear a place of social resort." More probably, white opposition was allayed by the general adherence of the colored riders to the unwritten rule that they take seats in the rear of the car. Whatever the explanation, the mixed cars caused little controversy. In December 1874, at the peak of a white effort to resegregate the public schools by mob force, rumors circulated that the streetcars were to be the next target. The negrophobic New Orleans *Bulletin* exhorted its readers, "We have now but one more duty to perform, and that is to secure a return to the system of star cars on our street railways." But despite the frenzy of white emotions, nothing was done and the cars remained integrated.

When the city streetcars were finally resegregated by state law in 1902, most white New Orleanians were altogether apathetic and a few even voiced their opposition to the measure. Bills demanding separate cars for white and colored passengers had been defeated in 1894 and 1900, after arousing strong protests from the railroad companies and some of the New Orleans newspapers. Profits, not philosophical egalitarianism, apparently motivated the railroad opposition. As the *Republican* had pointed out in 1874, the companies would not enjoy, "the soothing custom of sending two cars six miles to take home one colored and one white man late at night, when one car could do the service as well." The 1902 bill won passage only after its separate car provision was dropped in favor of one that separated the races by portable screens within the same car. Even so, the powerful *Daily Picayune* branded the bill, "a nuisance" and a number of white Orleanians expressed the opinion that the measure merely echoed local custom and threatened to incite antipathy between the races. But supported overwhelmingly by the rural representatives, the bill became law. Thirty-five years after the

Congo Square demonstrations, streetcar desegregation became the final casualty of the Negro crusade against the color line in New Orleans.

This prolonged, spirited assault against racial segregation in public transportation, by blacks, so soon after the Civil War, could have happened only in New Orleans. Prior to the Louisiana Purchase, in 1804, the territory was under the control of the French. During their administration, many blacks became wealthy and were educated.

One of the conditions of the sale of the territory to the United States was that the Creole population would not be subjected to the harsh segregation laws that controlled the blacks. Since many of the Creoles were black, the law was difficult to enforce.[2]

This combination of wealth, education and the relative freedom of Creoles who had never been enslaved, created an unusual set of circumstances that the black community exploited to its own advantage for many years. The blacks finally lost the battle to the racists in 1902, victims of the spreading evil of the Plessy v Ferguson decision of 1896.

In 1904, Negroes in Houston, Texas organized their own transportation network.[3] Negroes in Savannah, Georgia and in Chattanooga and Nashville, Tennessee, also experimented with setting up their own transportation companies. None of these companies survived.[4] Although there were other very early boycotts besides the ones in New Orleans and the other southern states, the Negro boycotts in Virginia stand out as being of primary significance, in the evolution of this form of protest. Beginning thirty-seven years after the New Orleans showdown and fifty-one years before Montgomery, Richmond was another victim that reflected the influence of the Supreme Court's Plessy v Ferguson decision of 1896. The Virginia story, extending from 1904 to 1906, as related by Meier and Rudwick,[5] is another chapter in the eternal struggle for freedom.

finds that the first Africans arrived in Virginia in the first part of the 17th century. Like many of the Europeans during that period, they were brought in as indentured servants. A quest for a more profitable economy by the ruling class demanded an increase in the labor pool at a lower cost. Unlike indentured servants of European origin, who were paid and could buy their way into the economy, those of African origin were forced into perpetual servitude, i.e., chattel slavery.

These victims resisted enslavement by every means at their disposal. Two Virginians who wrote pages of valor in the history of Virginia were Gabriel Prosser and Nat Turner. In 1820, another group met in Richmond to explore the possibilities of colonization elsewhere in the United States to escape the harsh racial climate of Virginia.

When the Civil War was over, twenty-five black delegates attended Virginia's constitutional convention (1867-1868), and teamed up with their liberal white colleagues to adopt six resolutions to facilitate the readmission of Virginia to the Union. One of these provided for: equal protection of all men before the courts and equal political rights in all respects, including the right to hold public office, and a system of public schools, "which shall give to all classes free schools and a free and equal participation in all of its benefits."

During their brief Reconstruction period of political power, Negroes helped to encourage a system of public education that led to the establishment of Virginia Union University in 1865. Under the sponsorship of the American Home Mission Society, Virginia Union, located in Richmond, provided a liberal, classical education for freedom rather than following the Tuskegee model. By the turn of the century, it was rated among the nation's first grade colleges for Negroes, along with Atlanta University, Fisk, Howard, and Morehouse colleges.

In 1868, Richmond's Negroes organized the Virginia Home

Building Fund and Loan Association. In 1875, they organized the Land and Financial Association. During this period they bought between 80,000 and 100,000 acres of land and began a program of entrepreneurship that would carry them beyond Reconstruction and well into the next century. Among these ventures was the launching in 1885, by John Mitchell, Jr.,[6] of the newspaper, *Richmond Planet*.

After Reconstruction, the former confederates, with the quiet assent of the Federal authorities, seized control of the southern state governments. By disfranchisement and the adoption of "black codes", the states were able to restore a racially oppressive society that approximated slavery in many sections of the south.

With the Supreme Court's seven to one decision in the Plessy v Ferguson case in 1896, the states were empowered to fulfill the prophecy of the lone dissenter, Justice John Harlan:

"The present decision... will not only stimulate aggressions, more or less brutal and irritating, upon the admitted rights of colored citizens, but will encourage the belief that it is possible, by means of enactments, to defeat the beneficent purposes which the people... had in view when they adopted the recent Amendments of the Constitution.... The destinies of the two races in this country are indissolubly linked together, and the interests of both require that the common government of all shall not permit the seeds of race-hate to be planted under sanction of law. What can more certainly arouse race-hate than state enactments, which, in fact, proceed on the ground that colored citizens are so far inferior and degraded that they cannot be allowed to sit in public coaches occupied by white citizens? This, as all will admit, is the real meaning of such legislation as was enacted in Louisiana."

It was under this federal authority that in 1904, the Virginia legislature passed an act which demanded the separation of whites and Negroes on passenger vehicles. In accordance with the Act, the Virginia Passenger and Power Company changed its seating pattern and announced its intention to inaugurate Jim Crow rules on its streetcar lines in Richmond, Manchester, and Petersburg, effective April 20, 1904.

John Mitchell, Jr., former Negro councilman, editor of the *Richmond Planet* and president of the Mechanics Savings Bank of Richmond, warned that Negroes "shall protest and protest. We shall agitate and agitate. We shall never willingly submit." He expressed the anger of the Negro community. In the *Planet,* Mitchell pointed out that this was not the Richmond that he knew where Negroes and whites lived together "harmoniously."

Responding to Mitchell's editorial, *The News Leader,* one of Richmond's daily newspapers, argued that streetcar segregation was a safeguard against racial amalgamation. Mitchell reminded his readers that Richmond Negroes and whites had been traveling upon the streetcars together for forty years with no problems.

Richmond's black community was deeply disturbed over the fact that the new law gave police powers, including the right to carry guns, to conductors and motor men. Another Negro press, *St. Luke Herald,* stated that the very dangerous power placed in the hands of hot-headed, domineering young white men would cause trouble when they order Negroes to, "this seat or that seat." Richmond's Negro leaders, mainly black ministers, met with officials of the streetcar company on April 7, 1904.

Richmond's Negro Baptist clergy, controlling twenty-eight of the thirty-seven black churches of the community, was an influential group. Included was the venerable First African Baptist Church and Virginia Union University, one of the finest Negro institutions of higher learning at that time.

The ministers agreed to cooperate with the streetcar lines' segregation policy, after S.W. Huff, manager of the Virginia Passenger and Power Company, offered his solemn pledge that the conductors would be instructed to be courteous.

Mitchell, however, through the *Planet* expressed strong disagreement and urged readers to seriously consider a boycott, "If the entire Colored population, or at least ninety percent of it would agree to make the sacrifice and walk for a year, the agony produced on the white man's nerve-center, which is his pocket, would tend to cause an amelioration of our condition." Mitchell sent out invitations to fifty or sixty prominent Richmond Negroes to attend a protest meeting, and at least two hundred showed up. Among them were five bank officials, four physicians, five insurance executives, two officials of benevolent organizations, one college professor, one attorney and three undertakers. Only a few clergymen attended.

Mitchell denounced the members of the Baptist Minister's Conference, saying that the streetcar company officials were not sincere and could have rescinded the segregation order if they had chosen to do so. One of the members of the protest committee, W.P. Burrell, president of the Richmond Baptist Sunday School Union, and general secretary of the United Order of True Reformers, a leading mutual benefit organization, decided not to go along with the other ministers and urged people to walk and to stand up for their self-respect and rights as citizens.

Dr. R.E. Jones, president of the Richmond affiliate of the National Business League, followed with, "a 'hot speech' denouncing the 'Jim Crow' Negroes whose acceptance of segregation only caused the white people to enact more of it. Others spoke in the same vein. Before adjourning, the group formed a permanent organization and named Mitchell as chairman. The next meeting would be a rally at True Reformers Hall on April 19, the day before streetcar segregation was to begin in Richmond, Petersburg, and Manchester.

Approximately six hundred Negroes filled the hall on that day, marking the official beginning of the Trolley Car Boycott. The meeting attracted even more physicians and professors from Virginia Union and bank officials, but fewer ministers. Mitchell urged the people to stay off the streetcars. For those who do ride, "they should obey the law, avoid arrest and sit in the rear."

Another speaker who made a lasting impression was Mrs. Patsie K. Anderson, manager of the Women's Union Grocery Company. She said, "Negroes usually talk too much. Don't say anything. But walk!"

An electrifying moment came with the announcement that the Negro owners of Richmond's four banks had agreed to provide the financial support for a Negro transit line. They declared that it would not be in competition with Virginia Passenger and Power Company and would have as, "its sole purpose a desire to promote harmony between the races."

Mitchell clearly had the backing of the leading executives and community people, as well as all six of the black newspapers — even those that were officially church periodicals. These included the well-known Mrs. Maggie L. Walker, head of the Independent Order of St. Luke, editor of the *St. Luke Herald,* and president of the St. Luke Savings Bank, and the Reverend Dr. W.L. Taylor, president of the United Order of True Reformers and of the True Reformers Bank.

In the face of all the boycott support, the Baptist ministers took pains to mitigate the effectiveness of the denunciations that they were 'Jim Crow' Negroes. In a letter to the daily press, they explained that the Colored clergy had not attended the mass meeting at True Reformers Hall because they thought it best to let the citizens hold their own meeting, "unmolested" by the pastors. Yet they continued to deny support to the boycott and their action was followed by the influential Baptist Deacons Association. Only those preachers identified with a business enterprise backed the boycott.

After the boycott began, the city's daily newspapers almost completely ignored it, except to pronounce it a dismal failure. To keep morale high, Mitchell, through the *Planet* reprinted encouraging comments from Negro newspapers from all over the south, such as the Fort Smith, Arkansas *Appreciation;* the *Baltimore Afro-American Ledger;* and the Mound Bayou, Mississippi *Demonstrator.*

Despite the bankers' earlier promise, the Negro transit line was not organized. Most of the boycotters walked. The more affluent among them used their own buggies or rode the vehicles owned by Negro hackmen. Several undertakers provided "bus" service, and many Negroes hitched rides on passing delivery wagons. Negroes who entered the streetcars almost always obeyed the new segregation rules. In the first six weeks of the boycott, only one Negro was arrested.

The white press continued to call the protest a failure. On May 20, the *News Leader,* opined that, "to all appearances the Negroes of Richmond have quietly acquiesced in the operation of the new streetcar laws." The Negro ministers in refusing to participate, seriously weakened the movement. Also, later Mitchell charged that the trolley company helped to destroy the boycott by giving free passes to a number of Negro leaders. Yet, in October 1904, a half year after the boycott began, the *Planet* declared that except for the hottest summer days, eighty or ninety percent of the Negroes were still avoiding the trolleys.

One of the victories that the Negro community could and did claim, was the bankruptcy of the transit company that operated the trolleys. The Negro press blamed the failure on the loss of patronage. As late as June 1905, Mitchell asserted that, "Hundreds have refused to return to the streetcars.... Some ride only when absolute necessity forces them. They use it to carry boxes and bundles, regarding this as a method to get even."

In 1906, the Legislature enacted a law requiring segregation on all trolley cars throughout the state. Subsequently, protests in the state of Virginia were more numerous than in any other state in the Union. The list included nearly every important city in the Old Dominion: Danville, Lynchburg, Portsmouth, Norfolk, and Newport News were among the cities where major protests occurred. As elsewhere, however, the boycotts ended mostly in failure.

Faced with this oppressive history and political climate, Montgomery's boycotters had to plan carefully, stand together, work courageously and pray unceasingly if they were to succeed where so many others had failed. In the meantime, the appeal of Mrs. Parks' conviction was derided on a technicality.

In private discussions, the MIA leadership had considered since mid-January, launching a more directed attack on bus segregation laws. Attorney Durr, continuing to provide behind the scenes advice to Gray and Langford, stressed that if the black community wanted to make a legal challenge to the segregation provision, the appeal of Mrs. Parks' conviction would not be a sufficient vehicle. The Alabama state court's delaying tactics would hinder them, and the conviction even might be voided if they showed that another seat was unavailable for Mrs. Parks.

Durr advised the MIA to file its own suit, in federal court, alleging that segregated bus transportation was unconstitutional, in light of the earlier Supreme Court decision in the Brown public school case. E.D. Nixon supported Durr's suggestion. Attorneys Gray and Langford, with further counsel from New York NAACP attorney, Robert L. Carter, began drafting the necessary documents. The case would be filed on behalf of Mrs. Aurelia Browder and four other women who were challenging the constitutionality of bus segregation. The case was filed in the United States District Court on Monday, February 16, 1956.

The one day hearing was held on May 11, before a three-judge panel: Federal Judges Richard T. Rives, Seybourn H. Lynne and

Frank M. Johnson, Jr. During the private deliberations which lasted three weeks, one judge was heard to ask, "Can you command one man to surrender his constitutional rights if they are his constitutional rights, to prevent another man from committing a crime?" On June 4, 1956, the United States District Court declared in a two to one decision, that the bus segregation law of Alabama and, by implication, the city bus lines segregation law, was unconstitutional.

On November 13, when the United States Supreme Court refused to review the decision, and thereby affirmed the lower Court's decision outlawing segregation on buses, Montgomery's city officials defiantly challenged the ruling, to no avail.

The boycott, already 343 days old at that time, could have been called off. In a magnificent display of dedication and discipline, the members of MIA continued the boycott for another 38 days until the federal decree reached Montgomery. The written mandate arrived in Montgomery on December 20, and on December 21, 1956, nearly thirteen months from the start, blacks returned to the buses.

SEVEN

Summary & Commentary

Retrospective study shows that the events of those 381 days of the boycott produced an episode in the long history of man's struggles for freedom that was decidedly unprecedented. Beginning at the moment of Rosa Parks' arrest on December 1, 1955, when a fellow passenger fled the bus to sound the alarm, until King's momentous speech the evening of December 5, 1955, and to the final chapter, there was never any serious doubt that this was an event whose time had come.

The foregoing account tells of the incredible sequence of events that made it all possible. From the outset, it was a movement that chose its own officers, raised its own funds and planned its own strategies to defeat its formidable foe.

In the beginning, the people were ahead of their leaders. Fortunately, with the prodding coercion of E.D. Nixon and the wise choice of Martin Luther King, Jr., to lead them, they got their house in order before it was too late. The moment of truth came during the afternoon of December 5, after it was clear that the boycott had been an outstanding success.

As we have seen, several cities in prior years, had experienced short-term bus boycotts that had fizzled out without changing the racist policies of the companies involved. Was this to be one of those or could it be expanded into a successful conclusion? Who was this new, unknown, untested young preacher who was being primed to lead the campaign? These and other questions were uppermost in the people's minds during the first days of the boycott.

120

Another cause of concern was the inevitable backlash of the white community. With full command of the police department, the court, the press, and a well-financed constituency, the odds against the black community were heavy indeed. Rosa Parks had provided the spark to start the conflagration. E.D. Nixon had poured on the gasoline when the flames began to flicker. Then, the ball was in King's court.

Despite the difficulties of settling into a new parsonage and the responsibilities of recent fatherhood, King rose to the call and cried out, "Here I am Lord, send me!" King had been on his way to Montgomery for a long time. From Morehouse College in Atlanta, he was sent to Crozer Theological Seminary, and then to Boston University. Finally he was sent to Montgomery's Dexter Avenue Baptist Church. At each stop along the way, he had acquired vital equipment for his future role as a world leader.

It all came together at the Holt Street Baptist Church on December 5, 1955. Although few who packed the church had ever seen King or heard him speak, there was no doubt after his speech that he was their leader. When he left the church that night, the reality of the Montgomery Bus Boycott was a foregone conclusion.

Just as the black leaders misread, at first, the early resolve of the masses of the black community, so did the white supremacists of Montgomery. During the entire 381 days of the boycott, they mobilized and manipulated all of the considerable resources at their command in a futile effort to break the will of the people and bring them down to shameful defeat. The people withstood the bombings, false arrests, unfair court decisions, unwarranted firing from work, ostracism, malicious rumors against white supporters and obscene telephone calls.

The fear that permeated the community, and understandably so, seemed not to hinder the activities of the participants. Because of the conditions under which black people lived, worked and played, their fears were justified. Simultaneously, there existed a staunch determination among black Montgomerians to look out for and protect each other.

Mrs. Portia Trenholm was still cautious in 1971. During a taped interview conducted by Charles H. Wright, M.D., she maintained a continued loyalty to the members of the WPC by refusing to give the name of the faculty member who allowed Robinson to enter the College's mimeographing room on December 1, 1955.

This was a full fifteen years after the incident. There still existed among the members of the WPC a firm bonding and continued observance of an unwritten agreement of loyalty and protection.

Throughout the area there were many workers, not previously named, who made substantial and meaningful contributions to the boycott movement. Professor Robert Williams assisted with transportation, often driving King and Abernathy; Gladys Black, musical director at Holt Street Baptist Church; Rev. R.J. Glasco, chairman of MIA finance committee; businessman and mortician, Clarence W. Lee, assistant treasurer of the MIA; Mrs. Josie Lawrence, and Mrs. Catherine N. Johnson, active members of the WPC; Mrs. Maude Ballou, King's personal secretary; Mrs. Martha Johnson, MIA secretary; Mrs. Hazel Gregory, MIA general overseer; Mrs. Inez Ricks, money-raiser for the MIA; Rev. Robert E. Hughes and Rev. Thomas Thrasher, white ministers and members of the Alabama Council on Human Relations and others.

The nation and then the world began to take notice of and to provide support to the Montgomery Improvement Association. Words of encouragement and the resources for enduring became a torrent of endorsement from all over the world. Edgar Keemer, M.D., of Detroit, who donated a new station wagon, was concerned about the transportation of the boycotters. Some sent money anonymously.

Although the Supreme Court's refusal to review the lower court's favorable decision on November 13, 1956, virtually ended the need to continue the boycott, the Montgomery Improvement Association leadership elected to continue until the official order reached the Montgomery officials. Thus the strike continued without a word of dissent, for another thirty-eight days. On December 21, 1956, segregation on intrastate public transportation came to an end.

The black people of Montgomery, Alabama had met the mandate issued by Supreme Court Justice Harlan in his bitter denunciation of his fellow justices for their 7-1 Plessy v Ferguson decision of 1896. With a voice heavy with anger, he anticipated the Montgomery Bus Boycott sixty years before it was brought to a successful conclusion:

"The Negro objects and ought never to cease objecting to the proposition that citizens of black and white races can be adjudged criminals because they sit, or claim a right to sit, in the same public coach, on a public highway."
It took 60 years but it was done.

The Montgomery Bus Boycott did more than provide a positive answer to the Supreme Court Justice's 60-year old call for action against racial segregation. It helped to launch a 10-year national struggle for freedom and justice, the Civil Rights Movement, that stimulated others to do the same at home and abroad.

Wishing to extend the work of the Montgomery Improvement Association, King and others called a meeting for January 10 and 11, 1957 at Martin Luther King Sr.'s Ebenezer Church in Atlanta, Georgia. Sixty leaders from twenty-two southern communities attended. Their first focus, after organizing and structuring decisions, was on transportation desegregation. The eager and favorable response and the recognition of the great need for help in the cities, spurred the decision to call a second meeting in New Orleans on February 13. Ninety-seven members from thirty-five communities in ten states were in attendance. All forms of segregation and voter registration were added as major objectives. The name, in order to reflect a broadened focus, was changed to the Southern Christian Leadership Conference.[1]

Although there were other very early boycotts besides the ones in New Orleans and in Virginia, the spin-offs from the Montgomery Boycott sent reverberations throughout the South and indeed, the world. "I had no dream that it could happen in Tallahassee," said the Reverend C.K. Steele.[2]

Rev. Steele was referring to Tallahassee's mass boycott that began just five months after the Montgomery protest got started. In many respects, the Tallahassee experience differed from that of Montgomery. First of all, it was a smaller city. According to the 1950 census, it had a population of 27,237; 9,373 of whom were black.

The boycott in Tallahassee began in May, 1956 when two women students from Florida A&M college refused to move from seats in the front section of a city bus to the rear. The student body at the college took mass action. On May 28, they met and voted unanimously to stay off the buses for the remainder of the school term.

The following day, students monitored the buses that passed through the campus and persuaded blacks not to ride them. Within a short time, word spread to the larger black community and the protest gained their support. With the approaching end of the school term, the question arose as to what would happen to the boycott when the students went home for the summer. Rev. Steele and other ministers solved that problem by agreeing to form an organization to keep it going.

Members of the community led by the ministers, held an organizational meeting and selected Rev. Steele as president.

They chose the Inner Civic Council (ICC) of Tallahassee as their name.

The mass movement that developed grew out of the deliberate efforts of the organizers, who mobilized the community through pre-existing organizations coordinated by ICC. It, too, provided a training ground for the further development of the strategy of nonviolence. Nonviolence became a disciplined form of mass struggle because it was systematically developed through organized structures of the movement.

As a result, the mass boycott put the buses out of business in the black community in Tallahassee. The leaders continued the boycott until the Supreme Court ruled in the Montgomery case. Then Tallahassee blacks resumed riding buses with desegregated seating.

Sparks that flew from the friction of this movement ignited flames of protest among Native Americans. During a public television program, "Making Sense of the Sixties," on January 27 1991, a Native American freedom fighter revealed that the civil rights struggles of African Americans gave his tribe the impetus to launch its own campaign for self-determination. These efforts have grown to the point that the Native Americans are now beginning to reject the autonomy of the Bureau of Indian Affairs and are demanding self-assertion through their own organizations.

Flames of dissent were ignited in far away places as well. In 1956 at the height of the Montgomery Bus Boycott, 20,000 African women marched to protest the enforcement of South Africa's oppressive pass-book law, to no avail. The festering abscess of discontent continued to grow until 1960, when it ruptured into what is recorded in history as the Sharpeville Massacre. Despite this and subsequent defeats, Africans have continued the struggle.

Those Africans, who led the mid-twentieth century fight to take back their countries from European colonialists were influenced by the United States' Civil Rights Movement. Some of the leaders, Ghana's Kwame Nkrumah, for example, attended schools in the United States and met protest leaders who supported their struggles for freedom when they returned home.

Although the Montgomery Bus Boycott grew to become an event of international significance, it began as a grass-roots, largely black action that was an interesting, informative and often dangerous interplay between the antagonists. In this author's view, the boycott was undoubtedly the wellspring of the Civil Rights Movement. It was not by any means, however, the first effort to desensitize a community. Nor, as you have read, was it the first long-running, sustained attempt to desegregate a transportation system. The primary distinction of the Montgomery Bus Boycott was that it had a distinct, dramatic beginning and a clear terminal point; a fixed date of conclusion. The benefits derived from the struggle were concrete and real.

Some of the previous boycotts, though introduced and sustained by dedicated and hardworking individuals and groups, were not as easily categorized as successful. Their accomplishments were often unseen and obscure. But, considering the milieu of the time, it is astounding that blacks such as John Mitchell, Jr., in 1904, in Richmond, Virginia, could lead the people through months and even years of hardship and indignation in an attempt to gain their rights.

Research revealed no evidence that Mitchell nor any of his associates, approached the state or federal court for relief at any time during 1904 conflict. This was unfortunate but understandable. Its onset was not started by an arrest but by an abrupt change of policy by the Trolley Company causing anger and consternation on the part of many of the previously loyal riders.

A question frequently asked is, "What made the Montgomery effort come together as it did, while the transportation boycotts in all other cities ended in failure? What made previously opposing forces in Montgomery mesh and blend into a fiercely determined and unified aggregation, able to resist and overcome the full arsenal of the opposition?"

The author tends to concur with the explanation set forth by Lerone Bennett, "Events of the previous years and the convulsion of the 50s had brought the people to the brink. They only needed an act to give them power over their fears, an instrument to hold in their hands and a leader to point the way."

Montgomery furnished all three — Rosa Parks' defiance, King, a remarkable fisher of men, and a new ideology, nonviolence. King solved the problem by clothing a national resistance movement in the disarmingly, appealing garb of love, forgiveness and passive resistance. As these all came together, it was evident that the time had come.

Then, too, this setting was primed, carefully and deliberately, by the efforts of the Women's Political Council and by the zealous and spirited efforts of Montgomery's Negro ministers. The clergymen set aside their disputes and discord and came together in a magnificent display of cooperation and fellowship.

Richmond's 1904 boycott was also a remarkable display of unity and cohesiveness. The community's skilled and unskilled workers and professionals joined forces without the involvement of the ministers, for the most part. The refusal of the ministers to give the boycott their full support was one of the reasons cited to explain its lack of success. The decisive role that ministers played in Montgomery supports that conclusion. The relationship between the dissenting ministers and the white community remained suspect among many of the disgruntled blacks in Richmond and elsewhere in Virginia.

The Civil Rights Movement in the United States, began as early as the seventeenth and eighteenth centuries. It would, of course, be impossible to relate the deeds and sacrifices of the "foot soldiers" throughout the many years of slavery and since that time. We have focused, therefore, on the bravery of a few including the enslaved Dred Scott, the brave Homer Plessy, the courageous students of Berea college and, indeed, the participants in the 1954 Brown v Board of Education case. But we see the people of Montgomery, Alabama as a glowing highlight of the movement. Instead of involving a few, an entire city of blacks rose up to fight the system to the bitter end without the direction or support of established leaders at the outset.

Although groundwork had been done previous to Rosa Parks' refusal to follow the bus driver's order, it was, beginning on the evening of December 1, 1955, that the community took up arms. The people were ready to take a stand. Fortunately, various persons assumed the role of leadership to guide the protesters through this ordeal.

The author hopes that this description of those fateful events of yesteryear will provide information and techniques that will help to ensure the success of those inevitable future struggles for freedom and justice, whenever and wherever the tocsin sounds.

NOTES

INTRODUCTION

1. Interview with Rosa and Raymond Parks, Leona McCauley and E.D. Nixon by Charles H. Wright, M.D., in 1970, on their roles in the Montgomery Bus Boycott. E.D. Nixon of Montgomery was, at the time, visiting the home of Mrs. McCauley and the Parks' in Detroit. Dr. Wright was able to spend considerable time with the four of them, taping their conversations and their responses to his questions.

2. *Alabama: A History,* by Virginia der Veer Hamilton, pp. 120-124. This book presents a detailed history of Montgomery beginning with a description of the city, long before it became Alabama's capital. It was the Black Belt's unofficial capital, hub of its political, economic, and social life. It shared this status, to some extent, with its satellite, Selma, another river town only fifty miles distant. Wilson's Raiders swept through the Black Belt in an 1865 raid, a minor skirmish in the war to free the slaves. Exactly one hundred years later, the march from Selma to Montgomery was an event of momentous consequence in the struggle for human rights. The author, Hamilton, asks the question, "Was it mere happenstance that Montgomery and Selma found themselves in the path of such events? Or, did their leadership and unyielding

defense of its life-style, shepherd them toward inevitable conflict and confrontation?"

3. *Alabama, A History,* p.123.

4. *The Chronological History of the Negro in America,* by Peter Bergman. The book contains an excellent compilation of facts dating from 1492 to 1968. The staff of compilers gathered yearly facts so that the reader has a sense of travelling through history. The arrival of Negroes to America and other countries, the enslavement, the revolts and the dates of all pertinent facts are set forth clearly and succinctly. The listings end around the time of the assassination, in Memphis, Tennessee, of Martin Luther King, Jr.

CHAPTER ONE

1. Plessy v. Ferguson 163 U.S. 537 (1896). Homer Plessy was arrested on the affidavit of two witnesses, charging him with violation of Act. No. 111, of the Laws of Louisiana, session of 1890, averring that he was, "a colored passenger on a train of the East Louisiana Railroad Company," who did, "insist upon going into and remaining in a compartment of a coach of said train which had been assigned to white passengers." Mr. Justice Brown, after stating the case, delivered the opinion of the Court. The case turned upon the constitutionality of an Act of the General Assembly of the State of Louisiana, passed in 1890, providing for separate railway carriages for the white and Colored races.

The Petition for the writ of prohibition averred that the petitioner was seven-eights caucasian and one-eight African blood; that the mixture of Colored blood was not discernible in him, and that he was entitled to every right, privilege and immunity secured to citizens of the United States.

The constitutionality of this Act is attacked upon the ground that it conflicts with both the Thirteenth Amendment of the Constitution, abolishing slavery, and the Fourteenth Amendment which prohibits certain restrictive legislation on the part of the states.

2. Thirteenth Amendment (Section 1). Neither slavery nor involuntary servitude except as a punishment for crime whereof the party shall have been duly convicted, shall exist within the United States, or any place subject to their jurisdiction.

3. Fourteenth Amendment (Section 1). All persons born or naturalized in the United States and subject to the jurisdiction thereof, are citizens of the United States and of the state wherein they reside. No state shall make or enforce any law which shall abridge the privileges or immunities of citizens of the United States; nor shall any state deprive any person of life, liberty or property without the due process of law; nor deny to any person within its jurisdiction the equal protections of the laws.

4. Jim Crow Laws. In 1875, Tennessee adopted the first Jim Crow law and the rest of the South rapidly fell in line. Blacks and whites were separated on trains, in depots, and on wharves. After the Supreme Court, in 1883, outlawed the Civil Rights Act of 1875, the Negro was banned from white hotels, barber shops, restaurants, and theatres. By 1885, most southern states had laws requiring separate schools.

5. Ku Klux Klan. The Knights of the Ku Klux Klan began to flourish after 1867. A powerful secret order, members

armed with guns, swords, or other weapons, patrolled some parts of the South, day and night, to obtain control over Negroes through maiming and murdering, and to establish white supremacy.

6. Dred Scott v. Sandford 19 How 393 (1857). This was the decision of the United States Supreme Court on a case concerning a slave named Dred Scott. In 1834, Scott's master had taken him from the slave state of Missouri to the free state of Illinois and later to the free territory of Minnesota. After four years, they returned to Missouri where Scott sued for his freedom on the grounds that he had lived in a free state. The case was in various courts for eleven years.

In March 1857, the United States Supreme Court ruled that a slave did not become free when he moved to a free territory. Furthermore, it declared that Negroes, "had no rights which the white man was bound to respect and that... people of African descent are not and cannot be citizens of the United States, and cannot sue in any court of the United States." Chief Justice Roger Taney, who handed down this decision, was a Maryland slaveowner. While the South enjoyed this victory for slavery, abolitionists in the northern states demonstrated against the decision. The hostility brought about by this decision took the North and South even closer to war.

7. Berea College v. Kentucky 211 U.S. 45 (1908); Loren Miller's *The Petitioners, the Story of the Supreme Court of the United States and the Negro.* The Kentucky legislature enacted a statute effective July 15, 1904, forbidding the maintenance of any school, college, or institution where persons of the white and Negro race are both received as pupils for instruction. The college clung to its principles and, as a corporation, was indicted,

convicted, and fined one thousand dollars for violation of the law. Kentucky's Court of Appeals upheld the statute, and Berea took its case to the U.S. Supreme Court. What happened to Berea in the Supreme Court is one of the most remarkable episodes in American jurisprudence.

8. *Eyes on the Prize,* by Juan Williams, p.62. The book has a chapter, "We're Not Moving to the Back of the Bus, Mr. Blake." It provides a full account of the Montgomery Bus Boycott, including feature pages on Jo Ann Gibson Robinson, Highlander Folk School and an interview with Mrs. Virginia Durr. Mrs. Durr continues to reside in Montgomery, Alabama. This author received a much appreciated communication from her in January 1991.

9. *Eyes on the Prize,* by Williams.

10. Brown v. Board of Education 347 U.S. 483 (1954). On May 17, 1954, the Supreme Court handed down its long awaited decision. Although the cases directly involved only South Carolina, Virginia, Delaware, Kansas, and the District of Columbia, the answer to the question of whether segregation of races was permissible under the Constitution affected a total of seventeen states and the District of Columbia that required segregation in public schools and four states that permitted segregation at the option of local communities.

In each of the cases, minors of the Negro race, through their legal representatives, sought the aid of the courts in obtaining admission to the public schools of their community on a non-segregated basis. In each instance, they had been denied admission to schools attended by white children under laws requiring or permitting segregation according to race.

11. *Voices of Freedom,* by Henry Hampton and Steve Fayer, pp. 1-15, Emmett Till, 1955, "I Wanted the Whole World to See." The book is subtitled, "An Oral History of the Civil Rights Movement From the 1950s Through the 1980s." It is based on an oral history archive comprising nearly one thousand interviews and is a thorough and interesting collection of stories of the Civil Rights Movement; and *Eyes on the Prize,* by Juan Williams, pp. 38-45.

12. *Voices of Freedom,* by Hampton & Fayer, p. 154. On June 11, 1963, Medgar Evers was returning home from a meeting in Jackson, Mississippi, where he was listening to a radio broadcast by President John F. Kennedy outlining legislation which was to become the Civil Rights Bill of 1964. As he pulled into his driveway, someone was stalking him. He left the car but did not make it into the house. His wife, Myrlie, heard the shots and found him face down, dead, at the doorway.

CHAPTER TWO

1. Rosa Parks, interviewed by Wright, 1970.

2. Rosa Parks, interviewed by Wright, 1970.

3. Rosa Parks, interviewed by Wright, 1970.

4. "Montgomery," unpublished paper by Dr. Lamont Yeakey, Columbia University, 1979, quoting *Odyssey,* by Earl and Miriam Shelby. Dr. Yeakey is a professor of History at the University of Wisconsin at Madison, and has written extensively on Montgomery, Alabama.

5. Interview with Rosa Park's friends, Mrs. Johnnie Carr and Mrs. Erna Dungee (Allen), on November 12, 1976, by Dr. Yeakey. He also refers to the Virginia Durr

Memoir, Vol. II, pp. 261-262, saying, "we discovered that the teachers taught the students not only things like domestic arts and reading, writing and arithmetic, but they imbued them with the whole idea of Americanism, the freedom of America, and the Bill of Rights and the Right to be free."

6. "Montgomery, by Yeakey, 1979, relates the early life of Rosa Parks and facts about her parents and grandparents.

7. "Rosa Parks," by Eloise Greenfield, *Ms Magazine,* August 1974, Vol. III, No. 2, p. 71.

8. *Eyes on the Prize,* by Williams, pp. 64-65; *The Origins of the Civil Rights Movement,* by Aldon D. Morris, pp. 139-157. Myles Horton attempted to assist the oppressed in overcoming their problems by training potential leaders. Persons from local communities dealing with the same problems were identified, brought to Highlander Folk School, and taught to analyze their situation in a group context. From the beginning, Horton envisioned HFS as an integrated institution, a rarity in the South of the 1930s. Horton's persistent attempts to attract blacks to come to the school usually went unrewarded. However, his dream finally materialized. In the 1940s and 1950s, those black people who for the most part were in situations where they weren't too dependent on white people began to attend. Otherwise, they would lose their jobs for coming. For that reason, Highlander attracted black ministers, funeral home directors, beauticians, people in unions, and independent small farmers.

Emotions and the lessons of racism usually determined the behavior of the newly integrated recruits who nervously entered Highlander for the first time. The staff members were trained to make these recruits comfortable by engaging them in music, songs and dance before entering the workshops. Blacks had to be convinced that they could trust whites at Highlander.

Black Protests, by Joanne Grant, p. 276, reports on Rosa Parks' visit to HFS in Monteagle, in March 1956, at the invitation of Myles Horton. It was one year after her first workshop experience; this time she was the center of attraction. She was asked to talk about her arrest and the boycott and to answer questions regarding her role. Horton asked Rosa why she did not move from her seat and what was her motivation. He wanted to know what went on in her mind. Rosa could only say that she wanted to know, "when and how could we ever determine our rights as human beings?" She explained about the bus driver's actions and said that was an imposition as far as she was concerned. Next, Horton wondered had she ever moved her seat before, when asked. Rosa said yes, she'd moved reluctantly. Usually, then, a Colored man would give her a seat, or she would stand. She added that those other persons had just gotten on the bus and she didn't think she should have to get up.

9. Author's conversation with Mrs. Johnnie Carr. During January 1991, by phone, Mrs. Carr discussed the sequence of events on that Thursday evening.

10. Author's conversation with Mrs. Carr, who related several such interesting anecdotes, dating back to the earlier days in Montgomery.

11. Nixon, interviewed by Wright, 1970.

12. Nixon, interviewed by Wright, 1970.

13. Nixon, interviewed by Yeakey, November 10, 1976.

14. L.D. Reddick, *Crusader Without Violence,* p. 112; "The Bus Boycott in Montgomery," in *Dissent,* Spring 1956, p. 108, by Reddick, quoted by Yeakey in, *Montgomery.*

15. Edgar N. French, "Beginnings of a New Age," in Glenford E. Mitchell and William H. Peace, III, eds., *The Angry Black South,* Corinth Books, New York: 1962, cited by Yeakey.

16. James Pierce, interview in the *Statewide Oral History Project,* Alabama, Vol. III, p. 1, cited by Yeakey.

17. E.D. Nixon, interviewed by Wright, 1970.

CHAPTER THREE

1. "Montgomery." E.D. Nixon interviewed by Yeakey on November 10, 1976; Statewide Oral History Project, Alabama.

2. "Montgomery." Rev. Abernathy, interviewed by Yeakey on October 20, 1976.

3. Abernathy, interviewed by Yeakey.

4. E.D. Nixon, interviewed by Yeakey.

5. *The Montgomery Bus Boycott and the Women Who Started It,* by Jo Ann Gibson Robinson, subtitled, "The Memoir of Jo Ann Gibson Robinson." It provides a first-hand account of some of the most significant and memorable contributions made prior to and during the early days of the boycott by the women of Montgomery, particularly members of the Women's Political Council.

6. "Trailblazers: Women in the Montgomery Bus Boycott," a paper prepared by Dr. Mary Fair Burks, is one of the several documents contained in the book, *Women in the*

*Civil Rights Movement - Trailblazers and Torchbearers,
1941-1965.* Dr. Burks presented her paper at the Second
National Conference on the Infusion of African and
African American Content in the School Curriculum, at
Georgia State University.

Dr. Burks recalls her own personal experiences during
the boycott, particularly her role with the Women's
Political Council. In addition, she provides descriptive
portraits of Rosa Parks and of Jo Ann Robinson, her
colleague at Alabama State College. Dr. Burks reminds
us of the need to recognize Robinson's contributions,
saying they should no longer be dismissed in a footnote,
an appendix or even in a paragraph or two. She calls
her the "Joan of Arc of the Montgomery Bus Boycott."

7. *Stride Toward Freedom,* by Martin Luther King, Jr., p.
   47. The book gives an account of King's life, primarily
   from 1953 to 1958. Its emphasis is on his role in the
   boycott and on his introduction to and study of the
   philosophy of Mahatma Gandhi.

8. Rosa Parks, interviewed by Wright, 1970.

9. "Montgomery," interview with Reverend Powell by
   Yeakey on November 17, 1976.

10. "Montgomery," by Yeakey, 1979.

11. *Alabama Journal,* December 3, 1955.

12. *Montgomery Advertiser - Alabama Journal,* December 4,
    1955. The two newspapers, the *Montgomery Advertiser*
    (the morning paper), and the *Alabama Journal* (the
    evening paper) were owned by the same family, a local
    publisher, R.E. Hudson, Sr. The *Advertiser's* editor was
    Grover Hall, Jr., and the *Journal's* editor was C.M.

Stanley. Only the *Advertiser* had a Sunday edition, but it was titled the *Montgomery Advertiser-Alabama Journal.*

CHAPTER FOUR

1. *Stride Toward Freedom,* by Dr. King; *Walls Came Tumbling Down,* by Rev. Abernathy. Abernathy's book is an autobiography which leads us through his association with Dr. King, through the boycott in Montgomery, and through the struggles of the SCLC. He writes of the protest marches in the South, in Washington, D.C. and in Chicago, Illinois. The epilogue discusses his relationship with President Jimmy Carter and the 1976 political campaign. He writes of wanting to take Andrew Young's place in Congress after Young resigned and accepted a position as Ambassador to the United States during the Carter Administration.

2. "Beginnings of a New Age," E.N. French.

3. Police Department of the City of Montgomery, Alabama Complaint against Fred Daniels, December 5, 1955, filed by officers R.M. Hammonds, and C.A. Weaver. Details of the complaint stated that when the bus stopped at the loading zone, a Negro female started to get on the bus, and Fred Daniels grabbed her and jerked her off.

4. *Alabama Journal,* December 5, 1955.

5. *Montgomery Advertiser,* December 1955.

6. *Stride Toward Freedom,* by Dr. King.

7. *Alabama Journal,* article by B. Honicker, December 5, 1955.

8. E.D. Nixon, interviewed by Wright, 1970.

9. Reverend French, along with Abernathy and Nixon, drafted the three proposals for the resolution.

10. Reverend Abernathy, interviewed by Yeakey, October 20, 1976.

11. Rufus Lewis, interviewed by Yeakey, November 15, 1976.

12. Reverend Abernathy, interviewed by Yeakey. Abernathy recalled the tension at the meeting and the importance of the decisions made at that meeting.

13. *Stride Toward Freedom,* pp. 56-57; *Walls Came Tumbling Down,* by Abernathy, p. 143.

14. Abernathy interview, October 20, 1976; Rufus Lewis interview, November 15, 1976.

15. Abernathy interview, October 20, 1976.

16. W.R. Miller, *Martin Luther King, Jr.,* p. 38, quoted in "Montgomery."

17. Rufus Lewis interview, November 15, 1976.

18. Fred Gray interviewed by Yeakey, November 18, 1976.

19. Rev. Dr. B.J. Simms, interviewed by Yeakey, November 30, 1976; *What Manner of Man,* by Lerone Bennett. Bennett's book is a biography of Martin Luther King, Jr., 1929 to 1968. Benjamin E. Mays writes in the introduction that the book is well-named, even though it is hardly possible for anyone to explain what it is that makes a man great and especially one who belongs to a submerged group subjected to denials and embarrassed by indignities. He writes that "It may be that only one man in ten million could have led the Montgomery Bus Boycott without that city exploding into one of the worst race

race riots in history." In writing the book, the author, Bennett, used materials collected in personal interviews with Dr. King, his wife, close friends, classmates and relatives. The author, as did Dr. King, graduated from Morehouse College in Atlanta, Georgia.

20. Reverend Abernathy interview, October 20, 1976.

21. E.D. Nixon interview, November 10, 1976: *Stride Toward Freedom,* p. 43; *Odessey,* by Earl and Miriam Shelby, quoted by Yeakey and his interview with Atty. Fred Gray.

22. *Parting the Waters,* by Taylor Branch, pp. 137-138. Branch has written "an epic of America" on the threshold of its most explosive era. He includes the years, 1954-1963. The chapters, "First Trombone," and, "The Montgomery Bus Boycott," give vivid details of King's involvement with the Movement.

23. *Stride Toward Freedom,* pp. 34-36; *The Origins of the Civil Rights Movement,* by Aldon D. Morris.

CHAPTER FIVE

1. Virginia & Clifford Durr, interview in *Statewide Oral History Project,* Vol. III, p. 21, quoted by Yeakey in "Montgomery."

2. Reverend A.W. Wilson, interviewed by Yeakey, November 29, 1976.

3. *Stride Toward Freedom,* by King; Interview with Reverend W.F. Alford, November 13, 1976.

4. E.D. Nixon interview in *Statewide,* quoted by Yeakey.

5. E.D. Nixon interviewed by Yeakey; and *Stride Toward Freedom.*

6. Eugene Ligon, a Montgomery businessman, quoted by Yeakey.

7. Rufus Lewis interviewed by Yeakey, November 15, 1976.

8. *Stride Toward Freedom,* pp. 61-62.

9. Rev. Abernathy interviewed, 1976; Resolutions that were composed by French, Nixon, and Abernathy.

10. E.N. French, *Beginnings of a New Age,* quoted by Yeakey.

11. L.D. Reddick, *the Bus Boycott,* p. 108, quoted by Yeakey.

12. *Stride Toward Freedom,* by King.

13. E.N. French, *Beginnings of a New Age,* p. 34.

14. L.D. Reddick, *The Bus Boycott,* p. 109.

15. *Bearing the Cross,* by David J. Garrow, pp. 52-54. Garrow's book is subtitled, "Martin Luther King, Jr., and the Southern Christian Leadership Conference." The author devotes the first chapter to the Montgomery Bus Boycott, starting on December 1, 1955, and concluding on the morning of December 21, 1956, when at 5:45 a.m., Mrs. Parks, Abernathy, Nixon, and Reverend Glenn Smiley met at King's home and boarded the first bus to come along.

16. Reverend Dr. B.J. Simms, interviewed November 30, 1976.

17. *What Manner of Man,* by Lerone Bennett, p. 73. Bennett states that the idea of an American Gandhi persisted. It was fueled by the glowing reports of Howard Thurman in the 1930s, who was then dean of the Howard University Chapel, and other Negroes who made pilgrimages to India and to Gandhi. In the turbulent forties, Asa Philip

Randolph electrified Negro Americans with a broad scale attempt to create a mass-based civil disobedience movement. Stimulated by John L. Lewis' successful sit-down strikes and massive unrest in Negro ghettos, Randolph called for a "nonviolent, goodwill, direct action campaign" including school and bus boycotts, mass marches on city halls and the White House. Buoyed by the response, Randolph staged in 1942, a series of meetings of a size and intensity unparalleled in the ghetto. But, due to violence erupting in America in 1943, the campaign failed and he was not able to put his plan into action.

18. *Walls Came Tumbling Down,* by Abernathy; Stride Toward Freedom.

19. *Stride Toward Freedom,* by King.

20. *Stride Toward Freedom,* by King.

21. *What Manner of Man,* by Bennett, p. 73.

22. *Stride Toward Freedom,* pp. 102-103.

23. *Bearing the Cross,* by Garrow, p. 68.

CHAPTER SIX

1. Fischer, Roger A. "A Pioneer Protest: the New Orleans Streetcar Controversy of 1867," in *Journal of Negro History,* 1968.

2. *Black Reconstruction in America, 1860-1880,* by W.E.B. Dubois, pp. 456- 471.

3. *Journal of Negro History.* "Transportation Segregation in Federal Courts Since 1865," pp. 174-191, July 1968.

4. Catherine Barnes. "Emergence of Jim Crow Transit." "Journey from Jim Crow." *Contemporary American History Series,* pp. 2-19.

5. August Meier and Elliott Rudwick. "Negro Boycotts in Segregated Streetcars in Virginia, 1904-1907," *Virginia Magazine of History and Biography,* 1973.

6. Logan and Winston, editors, relate the story of John R. Mitchell, Jr., (1986- 1929), born on the northern outskirts of Richmond, Virginia and who became a journalist, politician, banker and businessman. Mitchell managed to acquire an education, graduating in 1881 as valedictorian of the Richmond Normal and High School. After working as a teacher and a newspaper reporter, he assumed control of the *Richmond Planet,* in 1885, transforming it into one of the nation's leading Negro newspapers.

   In 1890, Mitchell, crusading against lynching, urged Negroes to purchase arms and to use them in their defense. "Great is the Negro!" he proclaimed. "Don't cringe and cower, stand up for your rights with manly dignity," he admonished. His attacks on lynching, Jim Crow and "ruinous race-legislation," plus his skill as a journalist, brought him great acclaim. The success with the *Planet* won him the presidency from 1890-1894, of the Afro-American Press Association.

   Mitchell served on the Richmond City Council from 1888 to 1896, but lost his seat in an election marked by open fraud. His political ambitions were constantly frustrated by powerful whites. His continued, outspoken participation caused problems with the white Republicans who refused to let him run for Congress in 1890.

   Mitchell then focused his attention on business and in

1902, founded the Mechanics Savings Bank of Richmond. He looked to economic betterment as a means of advancing his cause. He began to invest heavily in real estate, buying a movie theatre, a cemetery, and other business property in Richmond. As Grand Chancellor of the Virginia Knights of Pythias, funds were made available to him. The bank's assets remained small; but the four- story brick bank building, which he erected in 1910 in downtown Richmond, became a symbol of what a Negro might accomplish. In 1904, he was admitted as the first, and for many years the only, Negro member of the American Bankers Association. One casualty of his success was the *Planet,* which grew staid and respectable.

Mitchell, however, continued to speak out against racial injustice. During Virginia's Constitutional Convention (1901-1902), he wrote dozens of editorials attacking disenfranchisement. In 1904, as described in the text, Mitchell led the boycott of Richmond's newly segregated streetcars. In 1911, he lobbied against the ordinance requiring residential segregation in Richmond. The passage of the measure that year, profoundly depressed him.

During World War I, Mitchell's articles about the mistreatment of Negro soldiers led to the confiscation of the *Planet* by postal authorities. In 1921, he made one final and unsuccessful venture into politics: He ran for governor of Virginia, on what Negroes called a "lily-black ticket." The campaign was waged, not so much against the Democrats as against those white Republicans whom he saw as working against the Negro.

In 1922, the Mechanics Savings Bank went into receivership. Mitchell vowed he would save the bank and regain his good name, which he failed to do.

He died on December 3, 1929, at his home, 515 N. Third Street, Richmond, Virginia, after a brief illness. He was "virtually a poor man." He was buried in Evergreen Cemetery.

CHAPTER SEVEN

1. *Civil Rights, The 1960s Freedom Struggle,* by Rhoda Lois Blumberg. The book is subtitled, "Social Movements Past and Present." The section on the SCLC details its origin and many of its accomplishments throughout the years. Some who first rallied at SCLC and became familiar names: Bayard Rustin, who had joined others in the Journey of Reconciliation's early testing of southern interstate transportation and had spent twenty-two days in jail, at hard labor; Andrew Young, who would become an Ambassador to the United Nations under Jimmy Carter and serve as Mayor of the city of Atlanta.

2. Reverend C.K. Steele was selected first vice president of SCLC. He was very active with the organization and was upset when King designated Abernathy to succeed him as president in case he should be killed. Steele was not only a successful minister but a community leader and president of the Tallahassee NAACP. He helped to make the decision not to work through the NAACP with their bus boycott but to establish a separate organization as did Montgomery; and *Bearing the Cross,* by David Garrow.

BIBLIOGRAPHY

Abernathy, Ralph David. *And the Walls Came Tumbling Down.* Harper & Row Publishers, New York: 1989.

Alexander, Dr. Ann Field. "Between Two Worlds," pp. 120-125, *Virginia Cavalcade,* Vol. 40, No. 3. Virginia State Library & Archives: Winter, 1991.

Anderson, James D. *The Education of Blacks in the South, 1860-1935.* University of North Carolina Press, Chapel Hill: 1988.

Banks, James., and Cherry A. Banks. *March Toward Freedom: A History of Black Americans.* Fearon Publishers, Inc. California: 1974.

Barnes, Catherine A. "Journey From Jim Crow". "Emergence of Jim Crow Transit." *Contemporary American History Series,* New York: 1983.

Bennett, Lerone, Jr. *What Manner of Man.* Johnson Publishing Company, Chicago: 1976.

Bergman, Peter M. *The Chronological History of the Negro in America.* Harper & Row, New York: 1969.

Blaustein, Albert P. and Robert L. Zangrande, eds. *Civil Rights and the American Negro.* Washington Square Press, New York: 1968.

Blumberg, Rhonda Lois. *Civil Rights: The 1960s Freedom Struggle.* Twayne Publishers, Boston: 1984.

Branch, Taylor. *Parting the Waters: America in the King Years.* Simon and Shuster, New York: 1988.

147

Brooks, Thomas R. *Walls Come Tumbling Down: A History of the Civil Rights Movement, 1940-1970.* Prentice-Hall, Inc., New Jersey: 1974.

Burks, Dr. Mary Fair. "Trailblazers: Women in the Montgomery Bus Boycott," *Women in the Civil Rights Movement, 1941-1965,* eds. Vicki L. Crawford, Jacqueline Anne Rouse & Barbara Woods.

Chafe, William H. *Civilities and Civil Rights.* Oxford University Press, New York: 1980.

Civil Rights Education Project. "Free at Last, A History of the Civil Rights Movement and Those Who Died in the Struggle." The Southern Law Center, Montgomery: 1990.

Cushman, Robert F. *Cases in Civil Liberties.* Prentice Hall, Inc., New Jersey: 1986.

Dabney, Virginius. *Virginia, the New Dominion.* Double Day & Co., New York: 1971.

Dabney, Virginius. "Richmond: The Story of a City." "Moving Into a New Century."

Dubois, W.E.B. *Black Reconstruction in America, 1860- 1880.* Antheneum, New York: 1985.

Evers, Mrs. Medgar, with William Peters. *For Us, The Living.* Doubleday & Co., New York: 1967.

Fairclough, Adam. *To Redeem the Soul of America.* University of Georgia Press. Athens, Georgia: 1987.

Fischer, Roger A. "A Pioneer Protest: The New Orleans Street Car Controversy of 1867." *Journal of Negro History,* Vol. LIII, No. 3, July 1968.

Franklin, John Hope and Alfred A. Moss, Jr. *From Slavery to Freedom: A History of Negro Americans.* Alfred A. Knopf, New York: 1947 (1988).

Friedman, Leon, ed. *The Civil Rights Reader.* Walker & Company, New York: 1967.

Garrow, David J. *Bearing the Cross.* William Morrow & Co., Inc., New York: 1986.

Grant, Joanne, ed., *Black Protests.* St. Martin Press, New York: 1968.

Greenfield, Eloise. *Rosa Parks.* illus. by Eric Marlow, Crowell: 1973.

Hamilton, Virginia Van de Veer. *Alabama.* W.W. Norton & Co., New York: 1984.

Hampton, Henry and Steve Fayer with Sarah Flynn. *Voices of Freedom.* Bantam Books, New York: 1990.

Hurd, William B. "Public Transportation in Richmond," City of Richmond, Virginia: 1982.

Jarrett, Vernon. "The Forgotten Heros of the Montgomery Bus Boycott," Chicago: 1975.

Johnson Publishing Company, eds. *The Ebony Handbook.* Chicago: 1974.

Journal of Negro History. "Transportation Segregation in Federal Courts Since 1865."

Kennedy, Randall. "Reconstruction." *New Departures, Inc., Volume I, No. 2, 1990.*

King, Martin Luther, Jr., *Stride Toward Freedom, The Montgomery Story.* Harper & Row, San Francisco: 1958.

King, Martin Luther, Jr., *Why We Can't Wait.* Signet Books. New American Library of World Literature, New York: 1964.

Logan, Rayford Wand Michael R. Winston, eds. *Dictionary of American Negro Biography.* W.W. Norton & Company, New York.

Mason, Alpheus Thomas & William M. Beaney. *American Constitutional Law.* Prentice Hall, Inc., New York: 1972.

Meier, August and Elliott Rudwick. "Negro Boycotts of

Segregated Street Cars in Virginia, 1904-1907." *Virginia Magazine of History and Biography,* Virginia: 1973.

Meriwether, Louise. *Don't Ride the Bus on Monday, The Rosa Parks Story.* Prentice Hall: 1973.

Miller, Loren. *The Petitoners: The Story of the Supreme Court of the United States and the Negro.* Pantheon Books, New York: 1966.

Montgomery Advertiser, Montgomery: December 6, 1955.

Morris, Aldon D. *The Origins of the Civil Rights Movement.* The Free Press, Macmillan Publishers, New York: 1984.

Pfeffer, Paula F. *A. Philip Randolph: Pioneer of the Civil Rights Movement.* Louisiana State University Press, Baton Rouge: 1990.

Robinson, Jo Ann Gibson. *The Montgomery Bus Boycott and the Women Who Started It.* ed. by David J. Garrow. University of Tennessee Press, Knoxville, Tennessee: 1987.

Thompson, Leonard T. *A History of South Africa.* Yale University Press, New York: 1990.

Weisbrot, Robert. *Freedom Bound: A History of America's Civil Rights Movement. W.W. Norton & Co., New York: 1990.*

Williams, Juan. *Eyes on the Prize.* Viking Penquin, Inc., New York: 1987.

Witt, Elder, ed. "The Supreme Court and Its Work." *Congressional Quarterly, Inc.,* Washington, D.C.: 1981.

Wright, Charles H., M.D. "A 1970 Interview with Rosa & Raymond Parks, Leona McCauley and E.D. Nixon on their roles in the Montgomery Bus Boycott, 1955-1956," Cassette Tape.

Yeakey, Lamont. "Montgomery," Unpublished Manuscript, 1979.

INDEX

Abernathy, Ralph, 10, 13,
41-43, 53, 68-72, 76, 91-93,
122
Adair, Uretta, 50, 55
Adams, Thomas E., 102, 106
Alabama bus segregation
law, 2, 10, 35, 65-67, 118
Alabama Journal, 56, 59
Alabama State Board of
Education, 48
Alabama State College, 10,
13-15, 38, 43-46, 48, 57, 70
Alabama State Collegians, 48
Alexander, Cynthia, 50
Alford, W.F., 14, 82
American Home Mission
Society, 29, 46
American Missionary
Association, 29, 46
Anderson, Patsie K., 116
Arrington, Elizabeth, 50
Atlanta University, 13, 112
Azar & Campbell, 34
Azbell, Joe, 57

Bagley, J.H., 56, 57
Ballou, Maude, 122

Banks, Nathaniel, 99, 100
Baptist Ministerial Alliance,
11, 42
Barrett, Capt. W.B., 100
Baton Rouge, Louisiana, 15,
22-23
Beauregard, P.G.T., 103
Bell Street Baptist Church,
14
Benedict, U.S. Provost
Judge, 100
Bennett, Bruce, 32
Bennett, L. Roy, 12-13, 43,
52-53, 69-70, 73, 76, 82
Bennett, Lerone, 91-93, 127
Berea College v. Kentucky
(1908), 20-22, 127
Bethel Baptist Church, 11, 14
Beulah Baptist Church, 14
Bevel, James, 33
Billingslea, Orzell, 97
Black, Gladys, 122
Blake, James S., 2, 6, 7-8,
27, 66
Boston University, 11, 121
Brewer, David J., 20
Brooks, Sadie, 50

151

ABOUT THE AUTHOR

Roberta V. Hughes Wright (nee Greenidge) was born in Detroit, Michigan and has lived in the area all of her life. She holds a bachelor of science degree, a masters degree and a juris doctor degree from Wayne State University and a doctor of philosophy degree in behavior sciences in education, from the University of Michigan. She is a member of Alpha Kappa Alpha Sorority, a life member of the NAACP and a founder and ten-year member of the Board of Directors of the First Independence National Bank of Detroit.

Dr. Hughes Wright has a legal practice in Michigan and is also a member of the Bar of the District of Columbia. She has been admitted to practice before the Supreme Court of the United States.

Dr. Hughes Wright, a widow, with a daughter and son, is presently married to Charles H. Wright, M.D., a retired obstetrician and gynecologist, and founder of the Museum of African American History in Detroit.

Montgomery's Federal Courthouse across from Dexter Ave. Baptist Church

Alabama's Capitol (Montgomery) left
Dexter Ave. Baptist Church, right